REA: THE TEST PREP AP TEACHERS RECOMMEND

AP U.S. HISTORY
CRASH COURSE®

By Larry Krieger

Research & Education Association
Visit our website at: www.rea.com

Planet Friendly Publishing
✔ Made in the United States
✔ Printed on Recycled Paper
Text: 10%   Cover: 10%
Learn more: www.greenedition.org

GREEN EDITION®

At REA we're committed to producing books in an Earth-friendly manner and to helping our customers make greener choices.

Manufacturing books in the United States ensures compliance with strict environmental laws and eliminates the need for international freight shipping, a major contributor to global air pollution.

And printing on recycled paper helps minimize our consumption of trees, water and fossil fuels. This book was printed on paper made with **10% post-consumer waste**. According to the Environmental Paper Network's Paper Calculator, by using this innovative paper instead of conventional papers, we achieved the following environmental benefits:

Trees Saved: 9 • Air Emissions Eliminated: 1,835 pounds
Water Saved: 1,682 gallons • Solid Waste Eliminated: 542 pounds

Courier Corporation, the manufacturer of this book, owns the Green Edition Trademark. For more information on our environmental practices, please visit us online at **www.rea.com/green**

Research & Education Association
61 Ethel Road West
Piscataway, New Jersey 08854
E-mail: info@rea.com

AP U.S. HISTORY CRASH COURSE®

Published 2014

Copyright © 2010 by Research & Education Association, Inc. Prior edition copyright © 2009 by Research & Education Association, Inc. All rights reserved. No part of this book may be reproduced in any form without permission of the publisher.

Printed in the United States of America

Library of Congress Control Number 2009908565

ISBN-13: 978-0-7386-0813-6
ISBN-10: 0-7386-0813-0

LIMIT OF LIABILITY/DISCLAIMER OF WARRANTY: Publication of this work is for the purpose of test preparation and related use and subjects as set forth herein. While every effort has been made to achieve a work of high quality, neither Research & Education Association, Inc., nor the authors and other contributors of this work guarantee the accuracy or completeness of or assume any liability in connection with the information and opinions contained herein and in REA's software and/or online materials. REA and the authors and other contributors shall in no event be liable for any personal injury, property or other damages of any nature whatsoever, whether special, indirect, consequential or compensatory, directly or indirectly resulting from the publication, use or reliance upon this work.

All trademarks cited in this publication are the property of their respective owners.

REA Crash Course® and REA® are registered trademarks of Research & Education Association, Inc.

PART III: **KEY THEMES AND FACTS**

AP U.S. HISTORY CRASH COURSE TABLE of CONTENTS

PART I: INTRODUCTION

PART II: CHRONOLOGICAL REVIEW

PART IV: TEST-TAKING STRATEGIES

Online Practice Exam.................. *www.rea.com/studycenter*

ABOUT THIS BOOK

REA's *AP U.S. History Crash Course* is the first book of its kind for the last-minute studier or any AP student who wants a quick refresher on the course. The *Crash Course* is based upon a careful analysis of the AP U.S. History Course Description outline and actual AP test questions.

Written by an expert who has studied the AP U.S. History (APUSH) exam content for 20 years, our easy-to-read format gives students a crash course in the major ideas and events in U.S. history. The targeted review chapters prepare students for the exam by only focusing on the important topics tested on the AP U.S. History exam.

Unlike other test preps, REA's *Crash Course* gives you a review specifically focused on what you really need to study in order to ace the APUSH exam. Our review is broken down into specific topics and themes, offering you two ways to study the material – chronologically, or by key themes and facts.

The introduction begins with a discussion of seven keys for success and a glossary of 41 terms you absolutely, positively have to know. Part Two is composed of review chapters arranged in chronological order. Each chapter presents the essential information you need to know about important time periods in U.S. History.

The third section is made up of chapters devoted to key themes in American History, with particular attention focused on African American history and women's history. Finally, the *Crash Course* concludes with chapters that present strategies for successfully answering multiple-choice questions, the document-based essay question, and the free-response essays.

No matter how or when you prepare for the AP U.S. History exam, REA's *Crash Course* will show you how to study efficiently and strategically, so you can boost your score!

To check your test readiness for the AP U.S. History exam, either before or after studying this *Crash Course*, take REA's **FREE online practice exam**. To access your practice exam, visit the online REA Study Center at *www.rea.com/studycenter* and follow the on-screen instructions. This true-to-format test features automatic scoring, detailed explanations of all answers, and diagnostic score reporting that will help you identify your strengths and weaknesses so you'll be ready on exam day!

Good luck on your AP U.S. History exam!

ABOUT OUR AUTHOR

Larry Krieger earned his B.A. and M.A.T. from the University of North Carolina at Chapel Hill and his M.A. from Wake Forest University. In a career spanning more than 35 years, Mr. Krieger has taught a variety of AP subjects including American History, World History, European History, American Government, and Art History. His popular courses were renowned for their energetic presentations, commitment to scholarship, and helping students achieve high AP exam scores. All of Mr. Krieger's students scored above a 3, with most students scoring a 4 or a 5. In 2004 and 2005, the College Board recognized Mr. Krieger as one of the nation's foremost AP teachers.

Mr. Krieger's success has extended far beyond the classroom. He is the author of several widely used American History and World History textbooks, along with REA's AP Art History test preparation guide. In addition, he has spoken at numerous Social Studies conferences and conducts SAT and AP workshops around the country. His new venture, the *AP U.S. History Crash Course,* is the first of an innovative new series of test preparation books from REA that will help students strategically and effectively prepare for their AP exams.

ACKNOWLEDGMENTS

In addition to our author, we would like to thank Larry B. Kling, Vice President, Editorial, for his overall guidance, which brought this publication to completion; Pam Weston, Vice President, Publishing, for setting the quality standards for production integrity and managing the publication to completion; Diane Goldschmidt, Senior Editor, for editorial project management; Alice Leonard, Senior Editor, for preflight editorial review; and Weymouth Design, for designing our cover.

We would also like to extend special thanks to Mary O'Briant for copyediting, Ellen Gong for proofreading, and Kathy Caratozzolo of Caragraphics for typesetting this edition.

AUTHOR'S PEP TALK

Why write another AP United States History test preparation book? Bookstore shelves already contain a bewildering number of AP U.S. History (APUSH) books all claiming they will raise your scores. But will they really help you succeed? Do they provide you with the best information and the most useful strategies? I don't think they do. That is why I have written this book.

REA's *AP U.S. History Crash Course* is completely different from other test preps and study guides on the market today. Most APUSH test preps are often nothing more than slightly abridged versions of your textbook. The authors indiscriminately fill their books with facts, dates, Supreme Court cases, and endless acts of Congress for fear of leaving something out. In contrast, this *Crash Course* is deliberately selective. I don't include any extraneous information that is unlikely to appear on your exam. Instead, my targeted review chapters only focus on the important topics tested on the AP U.S. History exam.

The information presented in this book is based on a close study of all the released AP United States History exams. Contrary to popular belief, College Board test writers do not write questions on an unlimited number of topics. Their questions are designed to test key points on the Topic Outline contained in the College Board's United States History *Course Description* booklet. Because of this limitation, APUSH questions are actually focused on a limited number of key topics.

In short, this *AP U.S. History Crash Course* provides you with the information, tips, and strategies you need to succeed on the APUSH exam.

I have been teaching AP courses for more than 30 years, and all of my students have scored a 3 or above. If you take the time and study this book, you will also achieve a high score. So what are you waiting for? REA's *AP U.S. History Crash Course* will give you *"A Higher Score in Less Time—Guaranteed!"*

Larry Krieger

PART I:

INTRODUCTION

SEVEN KEYS FOR SUCCESS ON THE AP U.S. HISTORY EXAM

AP United States History textbooks are very thick and contain thousands of names, dates, places, people, and events. If all of these facts had an equal chance of appearing on your Advanced Placement United States History (APUSH) exam, studying would be a nightmare. Where would you begin? What would you emphasize? Is there any information you can safely omit? Or must you study everything?

Fortunately, preparing for the APUSH exam does not have to be a nightmare. By studying efficiently and strategically, you can score a 4 or a 5 on the exam. This book will help you understand and use the following seven keys for success:

1. **Understanding the APUSH Scale**

   Many students believe they must make close to a perfect score to receive a 5. Nothing could be further from the truth. Each APUSH exam contains a total of 180 points—90 from the multiple-choice and 90 from the free-response questions. Here is the score range from the 2006 Released Exam:

Score Range	AP Grade	Minimum Percent Right
111–180	5	62 percent
91–110	4	51 percent
76-90	3	42 percent
57–75	2	32 percent
0–56	1	31 percent

This chart is not a misprint. As is clearly shown, you can achieve a 5 by correctly answering just 62 percent of the questions and a 4 by correctly answering just 51 percent of the questions!

2. Understanding the APUSH Topical Outline

Many students believe that members of the APUSH exam development committee have the freedom to write any question they wish. This widespread belief is not true. APUSH test writers use a detailed topical outline that tells them what they can ask and what they cannot ask. Believe it or not, the topical outline is freely available. You can see it in the *AP U.S. History Course Description Booklet*.

Every question on your APUSH exam can be linked to a specific point in the topical outline. For example, many students were caught by surprise when the 2006 exam included a Document-Based Essay Question (DBQ) on Republican Motherhood. They should not have been surprised. Topic 5—"The Early Republic, 1789–1815"— specifically includes the topic, "Republican Motherhood and education for women."

3. Understanding the Importance of the Released Exams

The College Board has released APUSH exams for the years 1984, 1988, 1996, 2001, and 2006. In addition, they provided an online exam for all teachers who participated in the AP course audit. Taken together, these six exams contain 520 released multiple-choice questions. These questions can be used to understand the priorities and patterns of the APUSH test writers. For example, no specific dates and only three military battles (Saratoga, Antietam, and Pearl Harbor) have appeared on the exam. Instead, the questions cluster around highly specific topics such as the Monroe Doctrine and broad themes such as immigration.

4. Understanding the Importance of Key Topics

A content analysis of multiple-choice questions on the 2006 and 2001 released exams reveals important clusters of questions on these five key topics:

Topic	2006 Exam	2001 Exam
African American History	11 questions	21 questions
Key Terms	6 questions	5 questions
Women's History	6 questions	5 questions
Supreme Court Cases	5 questions	4 questions
Vietnam War	3 questions	2 questions

These five topics generated 31 multiple-choice questions on the 2006 exam and 37 multiple-choice questions on the 2001 exam. Since each multiple-choice question is worth 1.125 points, these five topics were worth 34.87 points on the 2006 exam and 41.62 points on the 2001 exam. Remember, you only need a minimum of 111 points to earn a 5 and 91 points to earn a 4. These five topics and the multiple-choice questions they generated would put you well on your way toward earning a 4 or a 5.

5. **Understanding the Overlap Between the Multiple-Choice Questions and the Free-Response Questions**

Both the multiple-choice questions and the free-response questions are taken from the topical outline in the *Course Description Booklet*. As a result, studying for the multiple-choice questions is tantamount to studying for the free-response questions. Most students fail to grasp the significance of this point. Since the multiple-choice questions are highly predictable, so are the free-response questions. The two types of questions are, in fact, highly related, since they both come from the same topical outline.

6. **Using Your *Crash Course* to Build a Winning Strategy**

This *Crash Course* book is based on a careful analysis of the *Course Description* topical outline and the released questions. Chapter 2 contains 41 key terms that you absolutely, positively have to know. Chapters 3–21 provide you with a detailed chronological review of key points derived from the *Course Description*'s topical outline. And finally, Chapters 22–32 give you detailed information about key themes and facts.

If you have the time, review the entire book. This is desirable, but not mandatory. The chapters can be studied in any order. Each chapter provides you with a digest of key information that is repeatedly tested. Acts of Congress, Supreme Court cases, and works of literature that have never been asked about have been omitted. Unlike most review books, the digests are not meant to be exhaustive. Instead, they are meant to focus your attention on the vital material you must study.

Focus your attention on building a coalition of topics that will generate the points you need to score a 4 or a 5. African American history, women's history, and the key vocabulary terms are the essential building blocks of any successful coalition. For example, these three topics generated 90 points on the 2006 exam—enough to earn a 4!

Although they are important, the great triumvirate (African American history, women's history, and key terms) is just the beginning. The Vietnam War (Chapter 32), key Supreme Court cases and trials (Chapter 26), and immigration and migration (Chapter 30) are very focused topics that typically generate three to five questions each.

Many students also find it useful to use the chronological chapters to concentrate on a specific period of time. Keep in mind that two essay questions are taken from before the Civil War, and two are taken from after the Civil War.

The multiple-choice questions are distributed as follows:

Pre-Columbian to 1789	20 percent or 16 questions
1790–1914	45 percent or 36 questions
1915–Present	35 percent or 28 questions

As you devise your chronological strategy, keep in mind that very few questions cover the period before the founding of Jamestown, and very few questions cover the period from

1970 to the present. If you are pressed for time, both periods can be safely skipped.

7. **Using College Board and REA Materials to Supplement Your** *Crash Course*

Your *Crash Course* contains everything you need to know to score a 4 or a 5. You should, however, supplement it with materials provided by the College Board. The *AP United States History Course Description Booklet,* the *2006 AP United States History Released Exam,* and the *2001 AP United States History Released Exam* can all be ordered from the College Board's Online Store. In addition, the College Board's AP Central site contains a wealth of materials, including essay questions, DBQs, and sample student essays from the past several years. And finally, REA's *AP U.S. History All Access* test preparation guide contains excellent narrative chapters, online quizzes and tests, and e-flashcards that supplement the *Crash Course* chapters.

KEY TERMS

I. COLONIAL AMERICA, 1607–1776

1. COLUMBIAN EXCHANGE

The Columbian Exchange refers to the exchange of plants and animals between the New World and Europe following the discovery of America in 1492.

New World crops such as corn, tomatoes, and potatoes had a dramatic effect on the European diet. At the same time, Old World domesticated animals such as horses, cows, and pigs had a dramatic effect on life in the New World.

2. MERCANTILISM

Mercantilism was the economic philosophy of Great Britain in the seventeenth and eighteenth centuries. Like other mercantile powers, Great Britain sought to increase its wealth and power by obtaining large amounts of gold and silver and by establishing a favorable balance of trade with its colonies.

3. HALF-WAY COVENANT

The Puritans established the Half-Way Covenant to ease requirements for church membership. The Half-Way Covenant allowed the baptism of the children of baptized but unconverted Puritans.

4. ENLIGHTENMENT

Enlightenment was an eighteenth-century philosophy stressing that reason could be used to improve the human condition.

Enlightenment thinkers such as Thomas Jefferson stressed the idea of natural rights. This can clearly be seen in the second paragraph of the Declaration of Independence:

"We hold these truths to be self-evident; that all men are created equal; that they are endowed by their Creator with certain inalienable rights; that among these are life, liberty, and the pursuit of happiness."

5. DEISM

Deism is the belief that God created the universe but allowed it to operate through the laws of nature. Deists such as Thomas Jefferson and Benjamin Franklin believed that natural laws could be discovered by the use of human reason.

6. THE FIRST GREAT AWAKENING

This term refers to a wave of religious revivals that spread across the American colonies during the 1730s and 1740s.

II. THE ARTICLES OF CONFEDERATION AND THE CONSTITUTION, 1776–1789

7. REPUBLICAN GOVERNMENT/REPUBLICANISM

The term *republican government* refers to the belief that government should be based on the consent of the people. Republicanism inspired the American revolutionaries of the eighteenth century.

8. SEPARATION OF POWERS

This term refers to the division of power among the legislative, judicial, and executive branches of government.

Alexander Hamilton defended the principle of separation of powers when he wrote, "There is no liberty if the power of judging be not separated from the legislative and executive powers . . . ."

9. CHECKS AND BALANCES

This term refers to a system in which each branch of government can check the power of the other branches. For example, the president can veto a bill passed by Congress, but Congress can override the president's veto.

III. BUILDING THE NEW NATION, 1787–1860

10. JUDICIAL REVIEW

The Supreme Court can strike down an act of Congress by declaring it unconstitutional. This principle was established in the case of *Marbury v. Madison*.

11. INTERNAL IMPROVEMENTS/AMERICAN SYSTEM

Internal improvements is a term referring to the development of a national transportation system.

The American System refers to a set of proposals designed to unify the nation and strengthen its economy by means of protective tariffs, a national bank, and internal improvements such as canals and new roads. Henry Clay was the chief proponent of the American System.

12. CULT OF DOMESTICITY/REPUBLICAN MOTHERHOOD

This idea refers to the idealization of women in their roles as wives and mothers.

The concept of "republican mother" suggested that women would be responsible for raising their children to be virtuous citizens of the new American republic.

13. TRANSCENDENTALISM

Transcendentalism was a philosophical and literary movement of the 1800s that emphasized living a simple life and celebrating the truth found in nature and in personal emotion and imagination. Ralph Waldo Emerson and Henry David Thoreau were the foremost transcendentalist writers.

14. PERFECTIONISM

Perfectionism was the belief that humans can use conscious acts of will to create communities based upon cooperation and mutual respect.

Utopian communities such as Brook Farm, New Harmony, and Oneida reflected the blossoming of perfectionist aspirations.

15. THE SECOND GREAT AWAKENING

This term refers to a wave of religious enthusiasm that spread across America between 1800 and 1830. Middle-class women played an especially important role in the Second Great Awakening by making Americans aware of the moral issues posed by slavery.

16. JACKSONIAN DEMOCRACY

This term refers to a set of political beliefs associated with Andrew Jackson and his followers. Jacksonian democracy included respect for the common sense and abilities of the common man, expansion of White male suffrage, appointment of political supporters to government positions, and opposition to privileged Eastern elites.

17. NULLIFICATION

Nullification is a legal theory that a state in the United States has the right to nullify (invalidate) any federal law that the state deems unconstitutional.

John C. Calhoun was the foremost proponent of the doctrine of nullification. Inspired by his leadership, a convention in South Carolina declared the tariffs of both 1828 and 1832 unenforceable in that state.

18. MANIFEST DESTINY

The term refers to the nineteenth-century belief that the United States would inevitably expand westward to the Pacific Ocean.

19. POPULAR SOVEREIGNTY

Popular sovereignty is the principle that the settlers of a given territory have the sole right to decide whether or not slavery will be permitted there.

Popular sovereignty led to a divisive debate over the expansion of slavery into the territories. The first great test of popular sovereignty occurred in Kansas.

IV. INDUSTRIAL AMERICA, 1865–1917

20. JIM CROW LAWS

These were post–Civil War laws and customs designed to discriminate against African Americans.

21. SOCIAL GOSPEL

Social Gospel refers to a nineteenth-century reform movement based on the belief that Christians have a responsibility to actively confront social problems such as poverty. Led by Christian ministers, advocates of the Social Gospel argued that real social change would result from dedication to both religious practice and social reform.

22. GOSPEL OF WEALTH

This was the belief that the rich were the guardians of society's wealth and, as such, had a duty to serve society in humane ways. Andrew Carnegie was the foremost advocate of the Gospel of Wealth.

23. SOCIAL DARWINISM

The term refers to the belief that there is a natural evolutionary process by which the fittest will survive. Wealthy business and industrial leaders used Social Darwinism to justify their success.

John D. Rockefeller used Social Darwinism to justify his success: "The growth of a large business corporation is merely survival of the fittest . . . the American Beauty rose can be produced in the splendor and fragrance which brings cheer to its beholder only by sacrificing the early buds which grow up around it. This is not an evil tendency in business. It is merely the working out of a law of nature and a law of God."

24. FRONTIER THESIS

This term refers to the argument by historian Frederick Jackson Turner that the frontier experience helped make American society more democratic. Turner especially emphasized the importance of cheap, unsettled land and the absence of a landed aristocracy. Here is an illustrative quote:

"From the beginning of the settlement of America, the frontier regions have exercised a steady influence toward democracy . . . American democracy is fundamentally the outcome of the experience of the American people in dealing with the West . . . ."

25. NEW IMMIGRANTS

This term refers to the massive wave of immigrants who came to America between 1880 and 1924.

The Old Immigrants came primarily from England, Germany, and Scandinavia. The New Immigrants came primarily from small farms and villages in Southern and Eastern Europe.

26. NATIVISM

Nativists favored the interests of native-born people over the interests of immigrants.

The Know-Nothings were the first nativist political party. Nativist's directed their hostility against Irish and German Catholic immigrants.

27. MUCKRAKERS

These were early twentieth-century journalists who exposed illegal business practices, social injustices, and corrupt urban political bosses.

Leading muckrakers included Upton Sinclair, Jacob Riis, and Ida Tarbell.

28. TAYLORISM

This was a system of scientific management developed by Frederick W. Taylor. Taylorism sought to develop a disciplined labor force by eliminating wasted motion.

29. VERTICAL INTEGRATION

Vertical integration occurs when a company controls both the production and distribution of its product. For example, Andrew Carnegie used vertical integration to gain control over the U.S. steel industry.

30. HORIZONTAL INTEGRATION

Horizontal integration occurs when one company gains control over other companies that produce the same product.

 ## V. BOOM AND BUST, 1917–1945

31. HOOVERVILLES

These were slums or shantytowns inhabited by unemployed and homeless people during the Great Depression.

32. LAISSEZ-FAIRE ECONOMICS

This is an economic philosophy stating that economic activities should be largely free of governmental interference, regulations, and restraint. It is interesting to note that laissez-faire economics was supported by leaders who, ironically, also supported protective tariffs.

33. ISOLATIONISM

Isolationism was a U.S. foreign policy calling for Americans to avoid entangling political alliances. During the 1930s, isolationists drew support from ideas expressed in Washington's Farewell Address. The Neutrality Acts of the 1930s were expressions of a commitment to isolationism.

VI. MODERN AMERICA, 1945–PRESENT

34. CONTAINMENT

Containment was the name for a U.S. Cold War foreign policy designed to contain or block the spread of Soviet influence.

George F. Kennan was an American diplomat and specialist on the Soviet Union who wrote an influential article advocating that the United States focus its foreign policy on containing the spread of Soviet influence.

35. McCARTHYISM

This term refers to the making of public accusations of disloyalty without sufficient evidence.

Senator McCarthy played on the fears of Americans by claiming that Communists had infiltrated the U.S. State Department and other federal agencies. Senator McCarthy's accusations helped create a climate of paranoia, as Americans became preoccupied with the perceived threat posed by alleged Communist subversives working in the United States.

36. DOMINO THEORY

This theory refers to the belief that if one country falls to Communism, its neighbors will also be infected and fall to Communism. For example, the fall of South Vietnam would lead to the loss of all of Southeast Asia.

The following statement by an American Secretary of State illustrates the domino theory:

"If Indo-China were to fall and if its fall led to the loss of all of Southeast Asia, then the United States might eventually be forced back to Hawaii, as it was before the Second World War."

37. MASSIVE RETALIATION

This was a military doctrine associated with President Eisenhower's secretary of state, John Foster Dulles. In the event of an attack by the Soviet Union or any other hostile power, the United States would retaliate with massive force, including nuclear weapons.

The threat of massive retaliation was designed to deter an enemy from launching an initial attack.

38. BLACK POWER

The Black Power movement of the 1960s advocated that African Americans establish control of their political and economic life. Key advocates of Black Power included Malcolm X, Stokely Carmichael, and Huey Newton.

39. HAWKS AND DOVES

Hawks supported U.S. involvement in the Vietnam War and believed America should increase military force to win the war. Doves opposed the Vietnam War and believed the United States should withdraw its forces from Vietnam.

40. DÉTENTE

The term refers to the relaxation of tensions between the United States and the Soviet Union; it was introduced by Secretary of State Henry Kissinger and President Richard Nixon. Examples of détente include the Strategic Arms Limitation Talks (SALT), expanded trade with the Soviet Union, and President Nixon's trips to China and Russia.

41. REAGANOMICS

"Reaganomics" refers to the economic policies of President Ronald Reagan; it is also called supply-side economics. President Reagan hoped to promote growth and investment by deregulating business, reducing corporate tax rates, and lowering federal tax rates for upper- and middle-income Americans.

PART II:

CHRONOLOGICAL Review

COLONIAL AMERICA
1492–1754

I. FIRST EUROPEAN CONTACTS WITH NATIVE AMERICANS

A. THE IROQUOIS CONFEDERACY

1. Political and linguistic differences hindered Native Americans as they attempted to respond to the threat posed by the European colonists.
2. The Iroquois Confederacy was the most important and powerful Native American political alliance. It successfully ended generations of tribal warfare.

B. TRADE AND THE COLUMBIAN EXCHANGE

1. The exchange of foods, plants, animals, and diseases between the Europeans and Native Americans is known as the Columbian Exchange.
2. Native Americans who interacted with the English became increasingly dependent on the fur-and-hide trade.
3. European diseases such as smallpox, influenza, and measles decimated the population of Native Americans.

C. SIMILARITIES AND DIFFERENCES BETWEEN NATIVE AMERICANS AND ENGLISH SETTLERS

1. Similarities included the following:
    ▸ *Both lived in village communities.*
    ▸ *Both shared a strong sense of spirituality.*
    ▸ *Both divided labor by gender.*
    ▸ *Both depended on agricultural economies.*

2. Differences included the following:

> ▶ *Native Americans did not share the English concept of private property.*
> ▶ *Native American children were often part of their mother's clan.*

II. THE PLANTATION COLONIES

A. THE VIRGINIA COMPANY

1. This was a joint-stock company.
2. The primary goal was to make a profit.
3. Religious motivation was much less important than in the founding of Maryland, Pennsylvania, Rhode Island, and Massachusetts.

B. TOBACCO

1. The introduction of tobacco cultivation made the British colonies in the Chesapeake region economically viable.
2. By the mid-1700s, tobacco was the most valuable cash crop produced in the Southern states.

III. THE PLANTATION COLONIES AND THE GROWTH OF SLAVERY

A. FROM SERVITUDE TO SLAVERY IN THE CHESAPEAKE REGION, 1607–1690

1. Indentured servants played a key role in the growth of the tobacco plantation system in Virginia and Maryland. They were the chief source of agricultural labor in both of these colonies before 1675.
2. Planters in Virginia and Maryland used the "headright" system to encourage the importation of indentured servants. Whoever paid the passage of a laborer received the right to acquire 50 acres of land. Masters thus enjoyed the benefits of this system.
3. The number of slaves increased dramatically in the last quarter of the seventeenth century.

4. Slave labor in colonial Virginia spread rapidly in the late seventeenth century, as Blacks displaced White indentured servants in the tobacco fields.

B. BACON'S REBELLION, 1676

1. Bacon's Rebellion exposed tensions between the former indentured servants, who were poor, and the gentry (the genteel class of planters), who were rich.
2. As planters became more suspicious of their former indentured servants, they turned to slaves as more reliable sources of labor.

C. GROWTH OF PLANTATION ECONOMIES AND SLAVE SOCIETIES, 1690–1754

1. Slavery developed and spread because the cultivation of tobacco required inexpensive labor.
2. Slavery was legally established in all 13 colonies by the early 1700s.
3. Although enslaved, Africans maintained cultural practices brought from Africa.
4. Rice was the most important crop grown in South Carolina during the mid-eighteenth century.
5. The Stono Rebellion (1739) was one of the earliest known acts of rebellion against slavery in America. It was organized and led by slaves living south of Charleston, South Carolina. The slaves tried to flee to Spanish Florida, where they hoped to gain their freedom.

IV. THE PURITANS

A. KEY FACTS

1. The Puritans came to New England in family groups. They wanted to escape political repression, religious restrictions, and an economic recession.
2. Their leader was John Winthrop.
3. The Puritans typically lived in small villages surrounded by farmland.

4. The typical Puritan community was characterized by a close relationship between church and state.

5. The Puritans believed in the necessity for a trained and educated ministry. They founded Harvard College and Yale College to ensure an adequate supply of ministers.

B. "A CITY UPON A HILL"

1. John Winthrop called on the Puritans to build a model society, which he referred to as "a city upon a hill."

2. The Puritans had a powerful sense of mission—to build an ideal Christian society.

3. The Puritans created a model Christian society with a strict code of moral conduct. For example, Puritans banned the theater.

4. Here is the full quote from Winthrop's famous sermon, in which he defined the purpose of the Puritan colony:

"For we must consider that we shall be as a city upon a hill. The eyes of all people are upon us. So that if we shall deal falsely with our God in this work we have undertaken, and so cause Him to withdraw His present help from us, we shall be made a story and a by-word through the world."

C. THE PURITANS AND RELIGIOUS FREEDOM

1. The Puritans immigrated to America for religious freedom. However, they did not tolerate religious dissent or diversity.

2. Not everyone shared Winthrop's vision. Both Anne Hutchinson and Roger Williams were expelled for challenging the Puritan authorities.

D. ANNE HUTCHINSON

1. She is best known for her struggle with the Massachusetts Bay authorities over religious doctrine and gender roles.

2. Hutchinson challenged clerical authority and claimed to have had revelations from God.

3. Massachusetts Bay officials banished Hutchinson to Rhode Island. She later moved to New York, where she and all but one of her children were killed by Indians.

Few Americans can identify Anne Hutchinson. She is most frequently remembered by New York motorists driving on the Hutchinson River Parkway and by tourists who admire her statue in front of the Boston statehouse. Hutchinson is a noteworthy example of a dissident who challenged the early Puritans. APUSH test writers admire dissidents and think you should know about them.

E. ROGER WILLIAMS

1. Roger Williams founded Rhode Island.
2. He advanced the cause of religious toleration and freedom of thought.
3. He believed that the state was an improper and ineffectual agency in matters of spirit.

F. THE HALF-WAY COVENANT

1. As time passed, the Puritans' religious zeal began to diminish.
2. The Half-Way Covenant eased requirements for church membership by allowing the baptism of the children of baptized but unconverted Puritans.

G. THE FIRST GREAT AWAKENING

1. Key points to remember about the First Great Awakening:
    ▶ *It took the form of a wave of religious revivals that began in New England in the 1730s.*
    ▶ *The wave soon swept across all the colonies during the 1740s.*
2. A key consequence was that "New Light" ministers advocated an emotional approach to religious practice; this weakened the authority of traditional "Old Light" ministers and established churches.
3. New Light ministers did the following:
    ▶ *Promoted the growth of New Light institutions of higher learning, such as Princeton*
    ▶ *Sparked a renewed missionary spirit that led to the conversion of many African slaves*
    ▶ *Led to a greater appreciation for the emotional experiences of faith*

> ▶ *Led to divisions within both the Presbyterian and Congregational churches, resulting in growing religious diversity*
> ▶ *Led to the growing popularity of itinerant ministers*
> ▶ *Led to an increase in the number of women in church congregations (Women became the majority in many church congregations.)*

Test Tip

*It is easy to allow the First Great Awakening to slip off your APUSH radar screen. Don't let that happen. The First Great Awakening has appeared on five of the six APUSH released tests. Pay special attention to reviewing the **consequences** of the First Great Awakening.*

V. PENNSYLVANIA AND THE QUAKERS

A. PENNSYLVANIA

1. The colony was founded by William Penn.
2. Penn created an unusually liberal colony, which included a representative assembly elected by the landowners.
3. Pennsylvania granted freedom of religion and did not have a state-supported church.

B. QUAKERS

1. Quakers were pacifists who refused to bear arms.
2. Quakers advocated freedom of worship and accepted a greater role for women in church services.
3. Quakers opposed slavery and were among America's first abolitionists.

VI. COLONIAL SOCIETY ON THE EVE OF THE REVOLUTION

A. KEY FEATURES

1. Northern merchants and Southern planters amassed great wealth. Nonetheless, colonial society did not have a hereditary aristocracy.

2. The number of non-English settlers continued to increase. For example, Scotch-Irish and German immigrants moved into Appalachia as the Native Americans were defeated.

3. The 13 colonies were religiously diverse. As a result of this religious pluralism, there was no single dominant Protestant denomination.

4. Slavery was generally accepted as a labor system. The institution was legally established in all of the colonies.

5. Functioning primarily as mercantile centers, colonial cities collected agricultural goods and distributed imported manufactured goods. Most colonial cities were ports that maintained close economic and cultural ties with England.

B. MERCANTILISM AND THE NAVIGATION ACTS

1. Mercantilism was England's dominant economic philosophy during the seventeenth and eighteenth centuries.

2. The goal of mercantilism was for England to have a favorable balance of trade. To achieve this goal, the colonies were expected to export raw materials and import finished goods.

3. Mercantilism was designed to protect English industry and promote England's prosperity.

4. The Navigation Acts were part of the British policy of mercantilism. They listed colonial products that could be shipped only to England.

5. The mercantilist system led to the subordination of the colonial economy to that of the mother country.

6. The North American colonies took advantage of Great Britain's policy of salutary neglect to work out trade agreements so they could acquire needed products from other countries.

C. WOMEN IN COLONIAL AMERICA

1. During the colonial period, a woman usually lost control of her property when she married.

2. During that period, a married woman had no separate legal identity apart from her husband.

3. During that period, single women and widows had the right to own property.

D. REPUBLICAN GOVERNMENT/REPUBLICANISM

1. Republicanism is the belief that government should be based on the consent of the governed.
2. Republicanism inspired eighteenth-century American revolutionaries.
3. Key principles include the following:
   - *Sovereignty comes from the people. Representation should therefore be apportioned, based on population.*
   - *A republic is preferable to a monarchy because it would establish a small, limited government that is responsible to the people.*
   - *Widespread ownership of property is the bulwark of republican government.*
   - *Standing armies are dangerous and should be avoided.*
   - *Agrarian life is both desirable and virtuous.*

E. COLONIAL LITERATURE

1. Anne Bradstreet (1612–1672) was the first notable American poet and the first woman to be published in colonial America.
2. Phillis Wheatley (1753–1784) was the first published African American poet. Her writing helped create the genre of African American literature.

AMERICAN REVOLUTIONARY ERA
1754–1789

I. THE ROAD TO REVOLUTION

A. THE FRENCH AND INDIAN WAR, 1754–1763

1. As a result of the French and Indian War, France relinquished its North American empire. England now dominated lands east of the Mississippi, as well as parts of Canada.
2. The French and Indian War was a pivotal point in America's relationship with Great Britain, because it led Great Britain to impose revenue taxes on the colonies.

B. THE PROCLAMATION OF 1763

1. The Proclamation of 1763 forbade British colonists to cross an imaginary boundary along the crest of the Appalachian Mountains.
2. The primary purpose of the Proclamation of 1763 was to avoid conflict between the trans-Appalachian Indians and British colonists seeking inexpensive land.

C. STAMP ACT, 1765

1. The act's primary purpose was to raise revenue to support British troops stationed in America.
2. The issues raised were these:
     ▸ *Does Parliament have the right to tax the colonies?*
     ▸ *Can Parliament truly reflect colonial interests?*
3. A debate was provoked over the issue, "no taxation without representation."
4. The act was important for the following reasons:

> ▸ *The colonists demonstrated their willingness to use violence rather than legal means to frustrate British policy.*
> ▸ *The British maintained that the colonies had no right to independence from parliamentary authority.*
> ▸ *Patriot leaders claimed that the act denied them their British birthrights.*
> ▸ *Many colonists believed they were entitled to all the rights and privileges of British subjects.*

    5. The act was repealed because of a colonial boycott of British exports.

D. THE COERCIVE ACTS, 1774

1. The Coercive Acts were Parliament's angry response to the Boston Tea Party.
2. They were designed to punish Massachusetts in general and Boston in particular. Massachusetts lost many of its chartered rights, and the Port of Boston was closed until damages caused by the Tea Party were paid.

E. "COMMON SENSE," 1776

1. "Common Sense" was a political pamphlet written by Thomas Paine.
2. The pamphlet was a strongly worded call for independence from Great Britain.
3. Paine opposed monarchy (he called King George a Pharaoh!) and strongly favored republican government.
4. Paine offered a vigorous defense of republican principles.
5. Paine's words helped overcome the loyalty many still felt for the monarchy and the mother country.
6. Paine used biblical analogies and references to illustrate his arguments.

F. ENLIGHTENMENT

1. Enlightenment is an eighteenth-century philosophy stressing that reason can be used to improve the human condition.

2. Enlightenment thinkers, such as Thomas Jefferson, stressed the idea of natural rights—an idea that can be seen clearly in the second paragraph of the Declaration of Independence: "We hold these truths to be self-evident that all men are created equal; that they are endowed by their Creator with certain inalienable rights; that among these are life, liberty, and the pursuit of happiness."

3. Benjamin Franklin and Thomas Jefferson were representative examples of American Enlightenment thinkers.

G. DEISM

1. Deism is the belief that God created a universe that is governed by natural law.
2. These natural laws can be discovered by the use of human reason.

H. THE DECLARATION OF INDEPENDENCE, 1776

1. The authors of the Declaration of Independence used the philosophy of natural rights, derived from the writings of John Locke.
2. The authors appealed to the sympathies of the English people.
3. They accused George III of tyranny.

II. THE REVOLUTIONARY WAR, 1776–1781

A. REASONS COLONISTS SUPPORTED THE WAR

1. The colonists believed that George III was a tyrant.
2. They believed that Parliament wanted to control the internal affairs of the colonies without the consent of the colonists.
3. They were convinced that British ministers and other government officials had a corrupting influence on the colonists.
4. They wanted greater political participation in policies affecting the colonies.

5. They resented the quartering of British troops in colonial homes.

6. They wanted to preserve their local autonomy and way of life from British interference.

B. THE FRENCH-AMERICAN ALLIANCE AND THE BATTLE OF SARATOGA, 1777

1. The Battle of Saratoga was important because it convinced the French government to declare war on Great Britain and openly aid the American cause.

2. French military and financial assistance played a key role in enabling America to win the Revolutionary War.

3. French leaders were not motivated by a commitment to republican ideals. Their primary motivation was to weaken the British Empire.

4. The French-American Alliance influenced the British to offer generous peace terms in the Treaty of Paris.

Test Tip

APUSH test writers rarely ask questions about battles, but the Battle of Saratoga is an exception. Although you are not expected to know the military tactics or commanders, you are expected to know the **consequences** *of this pivotal battle.*

C. THE TREATY OF PARIS, 1783

1. The treaty established America's new boundaries. The United States stretched west to the Mississippi, north to the Great Lakes, and south to Spanish Florida.

2. America agreed that Loyalists would not be further persecuted.

III. FROM THE ARTICLES OF CONFEDERATION TO THE CONSTITUTION

A. THE ARTICLES OF CONFEDERATION

1. The writers of the Articles of Confederation were cautious about giving the new government powers they had just denied Parliament.

2. Weaknesses in the Articles included the following:
  ▶ *A lack of authority to tax*
  ▶ *A lack of authority to exercise authority directly over the states*
3. The most important accomplishment was the Northwest Ordinance of 1787. That ordinance did the following:
  ▶ *Provided for the orderly creation of territorial governments and new states (Ohio was the first state admitted to the Union from the Northwest Territory.)*
  ▶ *Excluded slavery north of the Ohio River*
  ▶ *Supported public education*

B. SHAYS' REBELLION, 1786

1. The rebellion was sparked by the economic frustrations of Massachusetts farmers who were losing their farms because they could not pay debts in hard currency.
2. The leaders of Shays' Rebellion sought these changes:
  ▶ *An end to farm foreclosures*
  ▶ *An end to imprisonment for debt*
  ▶ *Relief from oppressively high taxation*
  ▶ *Increased circulation of paper money*
3. The leaders of Shays' Rebellion did *not* attempt to overthrow the government of Massachusetts.
4. Shays' Rebellion helped convince key leaders that the Articles of Confederation were too weak and that the United States needed a stronger central government.

C. THE FEDERAL CONSTITUTION

1. The Constitution was the result of a series of compromises that created a government acceptable to large and small states, as well as to free and slave states.
2. The following provisions were in the Constitution, as submitted to the states in 1787:
  ▶ *The separation of powers, which organizes the national government into three branches*
  ▶ *The authority of Congress to declare war*
  ▶ *A guarantee of the legality of slavery*

▶ *The creation of an Electoral College to safeguard the presidency from direct popular election*

▶ *Provision for impeachment of the President*

▶ *Provision for the presidential State of the Union message*

▶ *Provision for ratifying the Constitution*

▶ *Federalism*

▶ *A bicameral legislature, as created by the Great Compromise*

▶ *Enumeration of the powers of Congress*

▶ *The Three-Fifths Compromise (Slaves counted as three-fifths of a person for purposes of representation and taxation.)*

3. The following provisions were *not* in the Constitution, as submitted to the states in 1787:

▶ *A two-term limit for presidents*

▶ *Universal manhood suffrage*

▶ *A presidential cabinet*

▶ *The direct election of senators*

▶ *Guarantees of freedom of speech and of the press (added in the Bill of Rights)*

▶ *The right to a speedy and public trial (added in the Bill of Rights)*

▶ *The idea of political parties (The framers opposed political parties. They believed that political parties promoted selfish interests, caused divisions, and thus threatened the existence of republican government.)*

APUSH test writers often qualify their questions on the Constitution with the phrase, "as ratified in 1788." Remember, the Bill of Rights was not part of the Constitution, as ratified in 1788. As a result, guarantees of freedom of speech and press were not part of the Constitution when it was ratified. Always read each question carefully, paying special attention to qualifying phrases.

D. THE FEDERALIST PAPERS, 1787

1. Alexander Hamilton and James Madison wrote the Federalist Papers (sometimes known as *The Federalist*) to support ratification of the Constitution of 1787.
2. The prevailing conventional wisdom was challenged when Madison and Hamilton asserted that a large republic offered the best protection of minority rights. "In an expanding Republic," wrote Madison, "so many different groups and viewpoints would be included in the Congress that tyranny by the majority would be impossible."

E. ANTI-FEDERALISTS

1. Those opposed to federalism feared that a strong central government would become tyrannical.
2. Opponents of federalism did the following:
    ▶ *Drew support primarily from rural areas*
    ▶ *Argued that the President would have too much power*
    ▶ *Feared that Congress would levy heavy taxes*
    ▶ *Feared that the government would raise a standing army*
    ▶ *Believed that the new national government would overwhelm the states*
    ▶ *Argued that individual rights needed to be protected*

NEW NATION
1789–1824

 I. ALEXANDER HAMILTON'S ECONOMIC POLICIES

A. PURPOSE

1. The aim of Hamilton's policies was to do the following:
   - *Promote economic growth*
   - *Strengthen the new nation's finances*
   - *Give financial interests such as Eastern merchants a stake in the new government ("A national debt," Hamilton observed, "if it is not excessive will be to us a national blessing. It will be a powerful cement to our union.")*

B. PROPOSALS

1. Hamilton proposed to do the following:
   - *Establish a national bank*
   - *Adopt a protective tariff to raise revenue*
   - *Fund the national debt*
   - *Assume state debts incurred during the Revolutionary War*
   - *Tax distilled liquor to raise revenue*
   - *Expand domestic manufacturing*
   - *Subsidize domestic manufacturers* (Note: Congress rejected this proposal.)

C. CONTROVERSY WITH JEFFERSON

1. Hamilton favored a "loose" interpretation of the Constitution. He used the implied powers of the "necessary and proper" clause to justify his proposals. Hamilton believed that what the Constitution does not forbid, it permits.

2. Jefferson favored a "strict" interpretation of the Constitution. He believed that what the Constitution does not permit, it forbids.

II. WASHINGTON'S FAREWELL ADDRESS

A. THE WARNING

1. Washington warned Americans about the dangers of foreign entanglements.

2. "The great rule of conduct for us in regard to foreign nations," Washington advised, "is, in extending our commercial relations, to have with them as little political connections as possible. So far as we have already formed engagements, let them be fulfilled with perfect good faith. Here let us stop."

B. IMPACT ON AMERICAN FOREIGN POLICY

1. President Wilson's opponents would use Washington's Farewell Address to justify their opposition to the League of Nations.

2. During the 1930s, isolationists would use Washington's Farewell Address to justify their support of the Neutrality Acts.

Washington may have been "first in war, first in peace and first in the hearts of his countrymen," but he has not been first in the minds of APUSH test writers. With the exception of his Farewell Address, Washington has been largely ignored on the AP US History exam. In contrast, his Secretary of the Treasury, Alexander Hamilton, is an APUSH superstar. Almost all exams include at least one question about Hamilton's financial plans. Washington's successor, John Adams, only appears in conjunction with the quasi-war with France and the resulting Alien and Sedition Acts.

III. THE PRESIDENCY OF THOMAS JEFFERSON, 1801–1809

A. THE "REVOLUTION OF 1800"

1. The victory of Jefferson and the Democratic-Republicans marked the end of what has been called the Federalist Decade.
2. The election of 1800 has been referred to as a revolution because the party in power gave up power peacefully after losing an election.

B. KEY TENETS OF JEFFERSONIAN DEMOCRACY

1. The yeoman farmer best exemplifies virtue and independence from the corrupting influences of cities, bankers, financiers, and industrialists.
2. The federal government must not violate the rights of the states. This principle of "states' rights" is proclaimed in the Kentucky and Virginia Resolutions.
3. Freedom of speech and the press are essential rights, since governments must be closely watched. The Alien and Sedition Acts violated this principle.
4. The scope and activities of the federal government should be reduced. The President should practice republican simplicity.

C. THE LOUISIANA PURCHASE, 1803

1. The Louisiana Purchase had its origins in Jefferson's desire to acquire the port of New Orleans to provide an outlet for Western crops.
2. The failure of the French army to suppress a slave revolt in Haiti played a role in motivating Napoleon to sell the Louisiana Territory.
3. Purchasing the Louisiana Territory violated Jefferson's belief in a strict interpretation of the Constitution. As a result, Jefferson had to be pragmatic and do what was in the best interest of the country.
4. Jefferson hoped to perpetuate an agricultural society by making abundant lands available to future generations.
5. The Louisiana Purchase was America's largest acquisition of territory—even bigger than Alaska!

IV. THE MARSHALL COURT

A. BELIEF IN A STRONG CENTRAL GOVERNMENT

1. Chief Justice John Marshall believed that a strong central government best served the nation's interests.
2. Marshall opposed states' rights.

B. *MARBURY v. MADISON*, 1803

1. This case established the principle of judicial review.
2. The ruling gave the Supreme Court the authority to declare acts of Congress unconstitutional.

C. OPPOSITION TO STATES' RIGHTS

1. Under Marshall's leadership, the Supreme Court upheld the supremacy of federal legislation over state legislation.
2. For example, in *Dartmouth College v. Woodward*, the Marshall Court ruled that a state cannot encroach on a contract.

D. ECONOMIC NATIONALISM

1. Marshall was an economic nationalist who promoted business enterprise.
2. For example, in *McCulloch v. Maryland*, the court struck down a Maryland law taxing the Baltimore branch of the National Bank.

Test Tip

John Marshall has cast a long shadow across both American judicial history and the APUSH exam. Most exams have a question about **Marbury v. Madison** *and judicial review. It is also important to remember that Marshall was a proponent of a strong central government and an opponent of states' rights.*

V. THE WAR OF 1812

A. CAUSES

1. Causes of the war included the following:
    ▸ *British impressments of American seamen*

▸ *British interference with American commerce*
▸ *British aid to Native Americans on the frontier*

B. CONSEQUENCES

1. Consequences of the war included the following:
   ▸ *Contributing to the demise of the Federalist Party*
   ▸ *Intensifying nationalist feelings*
   ▸ *Promoting industrialization*
   ▸ *Advancing the career of Andrew Jackson*

VI. THE PRESIDENCY OF JAMES MONROE, 1817–1825

A. CLAY'S AMERICAN SYSTEM

1. Internal improvements referred to transportation projects such as roads and canals.
2. Henry Clay believed that new transportation links would promote trade and unite the various sections of the country.
3. Clay's "American System" called for tariffs to protect domestic industries and fund internal improvements.
4. Because of its dependence on agricultural plantations and slave labor, the South benefited least from the era of internal improvements.

B. AN ERA OF GOOD FEELINGS OR RISING TENSIONS?

1. The demise of the Federalist Party left the Democratic-Republicans in control of Congress and the presidency.
2. The illusion of a national political consensus was shattered by such contentious issues as protective tariffs, federal aid for internal improvements, and the expansion of slavery into the new territories.

C. THE MISSOURI COMPROMISE OF 1820

1. The Missouri Compromise settled the first major nineteenth-century conflict over slavery.
2. Maine entered the Union as a free state.

CHRONOLOGICAL REVIEW

3. Missouri entered the Union as a slave state, thus maintaining the balance between free and slave states in the Senate.

4. The Compromise closed the remaining territory of the Louisiana Purchase above the 36° 30′ line to slavery.

Feelings were not always so harmonious during the so-called Era of Good Feelings. Clay's American System and the Missouri Compromise of 1820 both generated heated debate. Both of these topics have also generated a large number of APUSH questions. Make sure you review the purposes of Clay's American System and the provisions of the Compromise of 1820.

D. THE MONROE DOCTRINE, 1823

1. The Monroe Doctrine was a unilateral declaration of principles that asserted American independence from Europe in foreign policy.

2. The Monroe Doctrine asserted that the political system in the Western Hemisphere is different and separate from that of Europe. (Note that this assertion is similar to the same point in Washington's Farewell Address.)

3. It warned European nations against further colonial ventures into the Western Hemisphere.

4. It promised that the United States would not interfere in the internal affairs of European nations.

5. The Monroe Doctrine was successful because of the power of the British navy.

THE
AGE OF JACKSON
1824–1840

 I. **KEY TENETS OF JACKSONIAN DEMOCRACY**

A. BELIEF IN THE COMMON MAN

1. The Jacksonians had great respect for the common sense and abilities of the common man.
2. Andrew Jackson was seen as a common man who represented the interests of the people.

B. EXPANDED SUFFRAGE

1. The Jacksonians dramatically expanded White male suffrage.
2. During the Federalist Era, caucuses of party leaders maintained discipline and selected candidates. During the Jackson administration, nominating conventions replaced legislative caucuses.

C. PATRONAGE

1. The Jacksonians supported patronage—the policy of placing political supporters in office.
2. Many Jacksonians believed that victorious candidates had a duty to reward their supporters and punish their opponents.

D. OPPOSITION TO PRIVILEGED ELITES

1. As champions of the common man, the Jacksonians despised the special privileges of the Eastern elite.
2. Special privileges were anathemas to a government dedicated to promoting and protecting the common man.

II. THE TARIFF OF ABOMINATIONS AND THE NULLIFICATION CRISIS

A. THE TARIFF OF ABOMINATIONS, 1828

1. The tariffs passed between 1816 and 1828 were the first tariffs in American history whose primary purpose was protection.
2. The Tariff of Abominations forced John C. Calhoun to formulate his doctrine of nullification.

B. THE DOCTRINE OF NULLIFICATION

1. Developed by John C. Calhoun, the doctrine of nullification drew heavily on the states' rights arguments advanced in the Kentucky and Virginia Resolutions.
2. In the *South Carolina Exposition and Protest*, Calhoun argued that a state can refuse to recognize an act of Congress that it considers unconstitutional.

C. OPPOSITION TO NULLIFICATION

1. In the Webster-Hayne Debate, Daniel Webster forcefully rejected nullification. Webster concluded with his great exhortation, "Liberty and Union, now and forever, one and inseparable."
2. Jackson's opposition to nullification enhanced his reputation as a strong President.

III. THE BANK WAR

A. JACKSON'S VETO

1. Jackson vigorously opposed the bill to re-charter the Second Bank of the United States (BUS).
2. Jackson believed that the bank was a bastion of special privileges. He argued that the BUS was beneficial to advocates of "hard money" and thus inimical to the interests of the common people who elected him.

B. CONSEQUENCES

1. Jackson supported the removal of federal deposits from the Bank of the United States.
2. Jackson's attack on the BUS caused an expansion of credit and speculation.
3. The number of state banks, each issuing its own paper currency, increased.
4. Jackson's war on the BUS was an important catalyst for the emergence of a competitive two-party system. The Whigs hated Jackson and supported Henry Clay and his American System.

IV. JACKSON AND THE FORCED REMOVAL OF NATIVE AMERICANS

A. *WORCESTER v. GEORGIA*, 1831

1. The Cherokees differed from other Native American tribes in that the Cherokees tried to mount a court challenge to a removal order.
2. In the case of *Worcester v. Georgia*, the United States Supreme Court upheld the rights of the Cherokee tribe to their tribal lands.

B. JACKSON AND THE CHEROKEES

1. Jackson's antipathy toward Native Americans was well known. In one speech he declared, "I have long viewed treaties with American Indians as an absurdity not to be reconciled to the principles of our government."
2. Jackson refused to recognize the Court's decision, declaring, "John Marshall has made his decision: now let him enforce it."

There are normally very few APUSH questions devoted to specific presidents. Andrew Jackson is the exception. Because of his pivotal role in the nullification crisis, the bank war, and the forced removal of Native Americans, a number of APUSH questions focus on Andrew Jackson and his policies. So while it is safe to skip John Quincy Adams and Martin Van Buren, it is important to study Andrew Jackson.

C. THE TRAIL OF TEARS

1. Jackson's Native American policy resulted in the removal of the Cherokee from their homeland to settlements across the Mississippi River.

2. The Trail of Tears refers to the route taken by Native Americans as they were relocated to the Indian Territory of Oklahoma.

3. Approximately one-quarter of the Cherokee people died on the Trail of Tears.

V. PLANTERS AND SLAVES IN THE ANTEBELLUM SOUTH, 1816–1860

A. KING COTTON

1. The following factors contributed to making cotton the South's most important cash crop:

   ▸ *The invention of the cotton gin, which made it possible and profitable to harvest short-staple cotton.*

   ▸ *Rich new farm land in the Deep South was opened to the cultivation of cotton. By 1850, the geographic center of slavery was moving southward and westward.*

   ▸ *The rise of textile manufacturing in England created enormous demand for cotton.*

B. SOUTHERN SOCIETY

1. It is very important to remember that a majority of White adult males were small farmers rather than wealthy planters.

2. The majority of White families in the antebellum South owned no slaves.

3. Nonetheless, a small minority of planters who owned 20 or more slaves dominated the antebellum South.

4. The cost of slave labor rose sharply between 1800 and 1860.

C. SLAVE SOCIETY

1. Slaves maintained social networks among kindred and friends, despite forced separations.

2. The dramatic increase in the South's slave labor force was due to the natural population increase of American-born slaves.

3. During the antebellum period, free African Americans were able to accumulate some property in spite of discrimination.

4. Although Southern legal codes did not uniformly provide for the legalization and stability of slave marriage, slaves were generally able to marry, and the institution of marriage was common on Southern plantations.

5. The majority of slaves adapted to the oppressive conditions imposed on them by developing a separate African American culture.

6. Slave revolts were infrequent. Most Southern slaves resisted their masters by feigning illness and working as slowly as possible.

VI. THE TRANSPORTATION REVOLUTION

A. NEW DEVELOPMENTS

1. Completed in 1825, the Erie Canal sparked a period of canal building that lasted until 1850.

2. Steamboats became widely used in the 1820s and 1830s.

3. The first railroad appeared in the United States in 1828. Within 30 years, the United States had built 30,000 miles of track.

B. CONSEQUENCES

1. The Erie Canal strengthened commercial and political ties between New York City and the growing cities on the Great Lakes.

2. Canals helped open the West to settlement and trade.
3. Steamboats dramatically increased river traffic while significantly lowering the cost of river transportation.
4. Like the canals, the railroads enabled farmers in the Midwest easier access to urban markets in the East.
5. Canals, steamboats, and railroads had the least impact on the South.

SOCIAL AND CULTURAL MOVEMENTS IN ANTEBELLUM AMERICA

I. THE ROLE OF WOMEN IN ANTEBELLUM AMERICA

A. THE CULT OF DOMESTICITY/REPUBLICAN MOTHERHOOD

1. American women could not vote, serve on juries, or perform other civic tasks. These restrictions raised the question of what role women should play in the new republic.

2. The concept of "republican motherhood" advanced the idea that women did have a vital role to play as wives and mothers. Proponents argued that women should be educated to rear their children to be virtuous citizens of the new American republic.

3. The republican mother should be concerned with domestic, family, and religious affairs.

Test Tip

Many students are surprised when they encounter APUSH questions on the cult of domesticity/republican motherhood. They shouldn't be. Most APUSH exams have one, possibly even two multiple-choice questions on this important concept. Test writers have used straightforward definitions, quotes, and even pictures to see if students can identify the cult of domesticity/republican motherhood. A recent APUSH exam devoted the DBQ (document-based essay question) to this topic.

B. FACTORY WORKERS IN LOWELL

1. During the first half of the nineteenth century, textile mills in Lowell, Massachusetts, relied heavily on a labor force of women and children.

2. During the 1820s and 1830s, the majority of workers in the textile mills of Massachusetts were young, unmarried women.

3. Prior to the Civil War, Irish immigrants began to replace New England farm girls in the textile mills.

II. CHANGING THE ROLE OF WOMEN IN ANTEBELLUM AMERICA

A. CHARACTERISTICS OF THE WOMEN'S MOVEMENT

1. The movement was led by middle-class women.
2. It promoted a broad-based platform of legal and educational rights.
3. It had close links with the anti-slavery and temperance movements.
4. Followers held conventions in the Northeast and Midwest but not in the South.

B. THE SENECA FALLS CONVENTION, 1848

1. The Seneca Falls Convention was organized and led by Elizabeth Cady Stanton and Lucretia Mott.
2. The "Declaration of Sentiments and Resolutions" issued by the Seneca Falls Convention demanded greater rights for women. The declaration's first sentence clearly stated this goal: "We hold these truths to be self-evident: that all men and women are created equal."
3. The Seneca Falls Convention called for women's rights in the following areas:
    ▸ *Women's suffrage*
    ▸ *Women's right to retain property after marriage*
    ▸ *Greater divorce and child custody rights*
    ▸ *Equal educational opportunities*

Test Tip

*It is important to know what reforms the Seneca Falls Convention called for. It is also important to know what reforms the convention did **not** call for. For example, the Seneca Falls Convention did **not** call for more liberal abortion laws or equal pay for equal work.*

C. DOROTHEA DIX

1. Dorothea Dix worked to reform the treatment of people with mental and emotional disabilities.
2. Dix was not involved in the women's rights movement.

III. ABOLITION AND ABOLITIONISTS

A. THE SECOND GREAT AWAKENING

1. The Second Great Awakening was a wave of religious enthusiasm, led by itinerant preachers such as Charles Finney and Lyman Beecher.
2. Finney achieved his greatest success in central and western New York. This area became known as the "burned-over district" because of the fervent prayer meetings held during the Second Great Awakening.
3. The Second Great Awakening played an important role in making Americans aware of the moral issues posed by slavery.

B. AMERICAN COLONIZATION SOCIETY

1. The American Colonization Society worked to return freed slaves to the west coast of Africa.
2. The American Colonization Society was primarily led by middle-class men and women.

C. WILLIAM LLOYD GARRISON

1. Garrison was the editor of the radical abolitionist newspaper *The Liberator* and one of the founders of the American Anti-Slavery Society.
2. In the first issue of *The Liberator*, Garrison called for the "immediate and uncompensated emancipation of the slaves."
3. Here is a famous quote published in the first issue of *The Liberator* on January 1, 1831: "Let Southern oppressors tremble . . . I will be as harsh as Truth and as uncompromising as Justice . . . I am in earnest—I will not retreat a single inch—and I WILL BE HEARD!"

4. Garrison's support of women's rights caused the American Anti-Slavery Society to split into rival factions.

D. FREDERICK DOUGLASS

1. Frederick Douglass was the most prominent Black abolitionist during the antebellum period.

2. Although best known as an abolitionist, Douglass championed equal rights for women and Native Americans. He often declared, "I would unite with anybody to do right and with nobody to do wrong."

Most APUSH students study Frederick Douglass, and a significant number have read portions of his autobiography. In contrast, many students only have a vague memory of William Lloyd Garrison. Be sure to update and sharpen your notes on Garrison. Although Frederick Douglass reigns supreme in textbooks and courses, APUSH test writers have written a number of questions about this fervent abolitionist.

E. SARAH MOORE GRIMKÉ

1. Grimké was one of the first women to publicly support both abolition and women's rights.

2. "I ask no favor for my sex," declared Grimké. "I surrender not our claim to equality. All I ask of our brethren is that they will take their feet off our necks."

IV. TRANSCENDENTALISM AND UTOPIAN COMMUNITIES

A. TRANSCENDENTALISM

1. Transcendentalism is a philosophical and literary movement of the 1800s that emphasized living a simple life while celebrating the truth found in nature and in personal emotion and imagination.

2. Henry David Thoreau and Ralph Waldo Emerson were the leading transcendentalist writers.

B. UTOPIAN COMMUNITIES

1. Utopians shared a faith in perfectionism—that is, the belief that humans have the capacity to achieve a better life through conscious acts of will.
2. The best-known utopian communities included Brook Farm, New Harmony, and the Oneida Community.
3. Utopian communities strove to escape the competitiveness of American life, regulate moral behavior, and create cooperative lifestyles.

V. CULTURAL ADVANCES

A. EDUCATION

1. *McGuffey Readers* were the best known and most widely used school books in the nineteenth century. Also known as *Eclectic Readers*, the books included stories, poems, essays, and speeches supporting patriotism and moral values.
2. Newspapers flourished during the first half of the nineteenth century.
3. Educational reformers worked to pass compulsory school laws, create more teacher-training schools, and use state and local taxes to finance public education.

B. THE HUDSON RIVER SCHOOL

1. The Hudson River School was a group of artists led by Thomas Cole, who painted landscapes emphasizing America's natural beauty.
2. The Hudson River School was America's first coherent school of art.

GATHERING STORM
1840–1860

I. MANIFEST DESTINY AND TERRITORIAL EXPANSION

A. THE RIGHT TO EXPAND

1. Manifest Destiny was the name given to the belief that the United States would inevitably expand westward to the Pacific Ocean.
2. Manifest Destiny was used to gain public support for American territorial expansion.

B. TEXAS

1. Texas became the Lone Star Republic in 1836.
2. Although he favored territorial expansion, President Jackson opposed the admission of Texas into the Union. Jackson feared that debate over the admission of Texas would ignite controversy over slavery.
3. Texas was an independent republic until 1845, because Americans were divided over the issue of admitting another slave state into the Union.

C. OREGON

1. During the 1844 election campaign, the slogan "fifty-four forty or fight" referred to Polk's promise to take all of the Oregon land under dispute between the United States and Britain.
2. The United States and Britain reached a compromise that established the northern boundary of Oregon at the 49th parallel.

D. THE MEXICAN WAR, 1846–1848

1. President Polk justified the Mexican War by claiming that Mexican troops had illegally crossed into American territory, where they attacked and killed American soldiers. Hostilities had thus been forced on the United States by the shedding of "American blood upon the American soil."

2. Led by Abraham Lincoln and supported by the transcendentalist writer Henry David Thoreau, Whigs opposed the Mexican War.

3. The Treaty of Guadalupe Hidalgo ended the Mexican War. Under the terms of the treaty, the United States gained California and New Mexico (including present-day Nevada, Utah, and Arizona, as well as parts of Colorado and Wyoming) and recognition of the Rio Grande as the southern boundary of Texas.

4. The Wilmot Proviso called for the prohibition of slavery in lands acquired from Mexico in the Mexican War.

5. Although the Wilmot Proviso never became federal law, it was eventually endorsed by the legislatures of all but one of the free states, and it came to symbolize the polarizing issue of extending slavery into the territories.

The Wilmot Proviso is so well known that it is easy to believe that it became a law. In fact, it did not. Although the House passed the Wilmot Proviso twice, the Senate rejected it. APUSH test writers use the phrase "passage of the Wilmot Proviso" as a tempting but incorrect answer. Note that the Wilmot Proviso did not support popular sovereignty.

II. THE COMPROMISE OF 1850

A. NEGOTIATIONS

1. Stephen A. Douglas, Daniel Webster, Henry Clay, and John C. Calhoun all played key roles in the negotiations that resulted in the passage of the Compromise of 1850.

2. Abraham Lincoln did *not* play a role in the negotiations that led to the Compromise of 1850.

B. PROVISIONS

1. Provisions of the Compromise of 1850 included the following:
   - *Admission of California as a free state*
   - *Abolition of the slave trade in the District of Columbia*
   - *Continued protection of slavery in the District of Columbia*
   - *Passage of a more stringent fugitive-slave act*
   - *Establishment of territorial governments in New Mexico and Utah, without an immediate decision on the status of slavery*

III. POPULAR SOVEREIGNTY AND THE KANSAS-NEBRASKA ACT, 1854

A. POPULAR SOVEREIGNTY

1. Senator Stephen A. Douglas was the leading proponent of popular sovereignty.
2. The principle involved was that the settlers of a given territory would have the sole right to decide whether or not slavery would be permitted there.

B. THE KANSAS-NEBRASKA ACT

1. The act proposed that the Territory of Nebraska would be divided into two territories—Kansas and Nebraska.
2. Their status as slave or free states would be determined by popular sovereignty.

C. CONSEQUENCES OF THE KANSAS-NEBRASKA ACT

1. The act did the following:
   - *Repealed the Missouri Compromise of 1820, thus heightening sectional tensions*
   - *Permitted the expansion of slavery beyond the Southern states*
   - *Led to a divisive debate over the expansion of slavery into the territories*

▶ *Ignited a bloody contest for control over Kansas*
▶ *Split the Democratic Party*
▶ *Sparked the formation of the Republican Party*

IV. THE DRED SCOTT CASE, 1857

A. THE RULING

1. Dred Scott was a slave and thus could not sue in federal court.
2. Under the Constitution, slaves were private property and thus could be taken into any territory and legally held there in slavery.
3. Slaves could not be taken from their masters, regardless of a territory's "free" or "slave" status.

B. THE CONSEQUENCES

1. The ruling invalidated the Northwest Ordinance of 1787 and the Missouri Compromise of 1820.
2. The ruling became a major issue in the Lincoln-Douglas debates.
3. The decision widened the gap between North and South, thus bringing them closer to war.

It is very important to remember which compromises, acts, and Supreme Court decisions restricted the expansion of slavery and which did not. The Missouri Compromise of 1820, the Kansas-Nebraska Act, and the Dred Scott decision all permitted the expansion of slavery beyond the Southern states. Although the Compromise of 1820 did restrict the expansion of slavery above the 36° 30' line, it allowed Missouri to enter the Union as a slave state.

V. THE ELECTION OF 1860

A. THE REPUBLICANS AND DEMOCRATS

1. Led by Abraham Lincoln, the Republicans accepted slavery where it existed but opposed the further extension of slavery into the territories.

2. The Democratic Party split. Northern Democrats supported Stephen A. Douglas and popular sovereignty. Southern Democrats supported John C. Breckinridge, the extension of slavery into the territories, and the annexation of Cuba.

B. CONSEQUENCES

1. Lincoln won the electoral vote but did not receive a majority of the popular vote.

2. Led by South Carolina, seven Southern states seceded from the Union.

CHRONOLOGICAL REVIEW

THE
CIVIL WAR
1861–1865

I. NORTHERN ADVANTAGES AND DISADVANTAGES

A. ADVANTAGES

1. An extensive railroad network
2. A strong industrial base
3. A superior navy
4. A larger population
5. An abundant supply of food

B. DISADVANTAGES

1. A shortage of experienced and skilled military commanders
2. A divided population that did not fully support the war

II. SOUTHERN ADVANTAGES AND DISADVANTAGES

A. ADVANTAGES

1. A defensive war fought on its home territory
2. A long coastline that would be difficult to blockade
3. An important cash crop in cotton
4. A group of experienced and skilled military commanders
5. A close economic relationship with Great Britain

B. DISADVANTAGES

1. A smaller population than the North
2. A smaller industrial base than the North

Chapter 9

III. THE BORDER STATES

A. IMPORTANCE

1. Strategic location
2. Important industrial and agricultural resources

B. KEY BORDER STATES

1. Kentucky
2. Maryland

IV. THE BATTLE OF ANTIETAM AND THE EMANCIPATION PROCLAMATION

A. THE BATTLE OF ANTIETAM

1. The Union victory persuaded England and France to remain neutral. While both European powers saw advantages in a divided America, they followed a cautious policy toward both the North and the South.
2. The Union victory enabled Lincoln to issue the Emancipation Proclamation.

> *The Battle of Gettysburg and Sherman's March to the Sea are pivotal events that played a key role in the Civil War. However, like other military battles, they are totally ignored by APUSH test writers. Lee, Grant, and Sherman will not appear on your exam. Antietam is the only Civil War battle you need to remember. Keep in mind that the Union victory convinced England and France to remain neutral while enabling Lincoln to issue the Emancipation Proclamation.*

B. THE EMANCIPATION PROCLAMATION

1. Lincoln delayed issuing the Emancipation Proclamation because he didn't want to antagonize slave owners in the Border States.
2. The North originally went to war to preserve the Union. The Emancipation Proclamation strengthened the Union's moral cause.

3. The Emancipation Proclamation rallied anti-slavery support in England and France.

4. The Emancipation Proclamation did not free slaves in the Border States.

5. The Emancipation Proclamation freed only the slaves in Confederate states that were still in rebellion.

Test Tip

It is important to focus on what the Emancipation Proclamation did and did not do. It did significantly enhance the Union's moral cause. However, it did not actually free a single slave. It was much stronger on proclamation than on emancipation. Slavery was legally abolished by the Thirteenth Amendment.

V. KEY POLITICAL ACTIONS DURING THE CIVIL WAR

A. CONGRESSIONAL ACTIONS

1. Congress established a national banking system to provide a uniform national currency.

2. Congress chartered two corporations—the Union Pacific Railroad and the Central Pacific Railroad—to build a transcontinental railroad connecting Omaha, Nebraska, with Sacramento, California.

3. Congress passed the Homestead Act of 1862, offering cheap—sometimes free—land to people who would settle the West and improve their property.

4. Congress passed high tariffs to protect American industry from foreign competition.

B. EXPANSION OF PRESIDENTIAL POWER

1. Lincoln found that the war required active and prompt presidential action.

2. Lincoln suspended the writ of habeas corpus for everyone living between Washington, D.C., and Philadelphia.

CHRONOLOGICAL REVIEW

RECONSTRUCTION AND THE NEW SOUTH
——————1865–1900

I. **THE RECONSTRUCTION AMENDMENTS**

A. **THE THIRTEENTH AMENDMENT, 1865**

1. Abolished slavery and involuntary servitude
2. Completed the work of the Emancipation Proclamation

B. **THE FOURTEENTH AMENDMENT, 1868**

1. Made the former slaves citizens, thus invalidating the Dred Scott decision
2. Provided for equal protection of the laws for all citizens
3. Enforced congressional legislation guaranteeing civil rights to former slaves

C. **THE FIFTEENTH AMENDMENT, 1870**

1. The amendment provided suffrage for Black males.
2. It stirred controversy among women's rights advocates.
3. Some women's rights supporters, including Lucy Stone, Julia Ward Howe, and Frederick Douglass, supported the amendment.
4. Other women's rights supporters, led by Susan B. Anthony and Elizabeth Cady Stanton, opposed the amendment. They advocated, without success, for a universal suffrage amendment.

II. RADICAL RECONSTRUCTION

A. CAUSES

1. Former Confederates were elected to Congress.
2. Black Codes were enacted in Southern states.
3. Race riots broke out in New Orleans and Memphis.
4. There were attempts in the South to undermine the Fourteenth Amendment.

B. PROGRAMS AND POLICIES

1. Military occupation of the South was permitted.
2. Punishment of Confederate leaders became policy.
3. Restrictions were placed on the power of President Andrew Johnson.
4. The House of Representatives impeached Johnson because he obstructed enforcement of the Reconstruction Acts.

C. ACHIEVEMENTS

1. Public school systems in the Southern states were improved.
2. African Americans were elected to the House and Senate.

III. THE PLIGHT OF AFRICAN AMERICANS

A. FROM SLAVES TO SHARECROPPERS

1. The majority of freedmen entered sharecropping arrangements with their former masters.
2. Sharecropping led to a cycle of debt and depression for Southern tenant farmers.
3. The freedmen did not receive 40 acres and a mule.

B. BLACK CODES

1. The codes were passed by Southern state legislatures.
2. They were intended to place limits on the socioeconomic opportunities and freedoms open to Black people.
3. The codes forced Black Americans to work under conditions that closely resembled slavery.

IV. THE ELECTION OF 1876 AND THE COMPROMISE OF 1877

A. THE ELECTION OF 1876

1. Samuel J. Tilden polled more popular votes than Rutherford B. Hayes.
2. Tilden won 184 of the 185 electoral votes needed for election.
3. There were 20 disputed votes in four states, 3 of which were in the South.

B. THE COMPROMISE OF 1877

1. The Democrats agreed that Hayes would take office.
2. The Republicans agreed to withdraw all federal troops from the South.
3. Hayes promised to appoint at least one Southerner to his cabinet.
4. The Republicans agreed to support internal improvements in the South.
5. The Republicans abandoned their commitment to racial equality. For example, the Civil Rights Act of 1875 guaranteed equal accommodations in public places and prohibited racial discrimination in jury selection. The law was not enforced.
6. The Compromise of 1877 ended Congressional Reconstruction.

V. THE RISE OF JIM CROW SEGREGATION

A. THE 1883 CIVIL RIGHTS CASES

1. The cases weakened the protections given to African Americans under the Fourteenth Amendment.
2. Much of the Civil Rights Act of 1875 was declared unconstitutional.
3. The cases declared that the Fourteenth Amendment prohibited only government violations of civil rights, not the denial of civil rights to individuals.

B. *PLESSY v. FERGUSON,* 1896

1. The case involved a dispute over the legality of segregated railroad cars in Louisiana.
2. It upheld segregation by approving "separate but equal" accommodations for African Americans.
3. It led to the establishment of separate school systems for African Americans.
4. The doctrine of "separate but equal" was reversed in 1954 by the landmark decision in *Brown v. Board of Education of Topeka.*

Plessy v. Ferguson *and* Brown v. Board of Education of Topeka *are two of the most important Supreme Court cases in American history. APUSH test writers recognize their significance and have included at least one question about these cases on each of the released exams.*

C. DISENFRANCHISING BLACK VOTERS

1. Literacy tests and poll taxes were used to deny African Americans the ballot.
2. The grandfather clause exempted from these requirements anyone whose forebear had voted in 1860. Needless to say, Black slaves had not voted at that time.
3. Electoral districts were gerrymandered to favor the Democratic Party.

VI. BOOKER T. WASHINGTON

A. ATLANTA COMPROMISE SPEECH, 1895

1. Booker T. Washington called on African Americans to seek economic opportunities rather than political rights.
2. Washington declared, "In all things purely social we can be as separate as the fingers, yet one as the hand in all things essential to mutual progress."

B. KEY POSITIONS

1. Washington supported Black economic self-help.
2. Washington supported accommodation to White society.

3. Washington supported vocational education.
4. Washington supported racial solidarity.
5. Washington opposed public political agitation.

VII. THE NEW SOUTH

A. ECONOMIC DEVELOPMENT

1. Proponents of the New South supported building a more diversified Southern economy.
2. New South advocates championed the expansion of Southern industry.

B. POLITICAL REPRESSION OF AFRICAN AMERICANS

1. New South advocates supported the return of White conservatives to political power.
2. New South advocates supported the withdrawal of federal troops while ignoring the rise of the Ku Klux Klan and the increase in lynching.
3. African Americans who migrated to Kansas were known as Exodusters.

THE
OLD WEST
—— 1865–1900

 I. **THE TRANSCONTINENTAL RAILROADS**

A. CONSTRUCTION

1. The first transcontinental railroad was completed in 1869.
2. Five transcontinental railroads were constructed during the nineteenth century.
3. Irish and Chinese workers played key roles in the construction of the transcontinental railroads.

B. CONSEQUENCES FOR THE GREAT PLAINS

1. The railroads played a key role in the near-extinction of the buffalo herds. This dealt a devastating blow to the culture of the Plains Indians.
2. The railroads brought a tidal wave of troops, farmers, miners, and cattlemen to the Great Plains.
3. As the settlers built farms, range-fed cattle rapidly replaced the now decimated buffalo herds.

II. **THE TRANSFORMATION OF THE PLAINS INDIANS**

A. KEY CAUSES

1. The virtual extermination of the buffalo doomed the Plains Indians' nomadic way of life.
2. The Plains Indians were ravaged by diseases.
3. The transcontinental railroads transformed the economy of the entire region.

Chapter 11

B. PUBLICATION OF *CENTURY OF DISHONOR,* 1881

1. The book was written by Helen Hunt Jackson.
2. It aroused public awareness of the federal government's long record of betraying and cheating Native Americans.

C. THE DAWES ACT OF 1887

1. Goals
   ▶ *Inspired in part by* Century of Dishonor, *the Dawes Act was a misguided attempt to reform the government's Native American policy.*
   ▶ *The legislation's goal was to assimilate Native Americans into the mainstream of American life by dissolving tribes as legal entities and eliminating tribal ownership of land.*
2. Consequences
   ▶ *The Dawes Act ignored the inherent reliance of traditional Indian culture on tribally owned land.*
   ▶ *By 1900, Indians had lost 50 percent of the 156 million acres they had held just two decades earlier.*
   ▶ *The forced-assimilation doctrine of the Dawes Act remained the cornerstone of the government's official Indian policy for nearly half a century.*
   ▶ *The Indian Reorganization Act of 1934 partially reversed the individualistic approach of the Dawes Act by restoring the tribal basis of Indian life.*

D. THE GHOST DANCE

1. The dance was a sacred ritual expressing a vision that the buffalo would return and White civilization would vanish.
2. The army attempted to destroy it at the so-called Battle of Wounded Knee in 1890, fearing that the ceremony would cause an uprising.
3. As many as 200 Indian men, women, and children were killed at the Battle of Wounded Knee.

III. THE FADING FRONTIER

A. A WATERSHED REPORT

1. In 1890, the superintendent of the census reported that for the first time in American history a frontier line no longer existed.
2. The "closing" of the frontier inspired Frederick Jackson Turner to write one of the most influential essays in American history—"The Significance of the Frontier in American History."

B. AN INFLUENTIAL THESIS

1. Turner argued that the existence of cheap, unsettled land had played a key role in making American society more democratic.
2. The frontier helped shape a distinctive American spirit of democracy and egalitarianism.
3. The frontier acted as a safety valve that enabled Eastern factory workers and immigrants to escape bad economic conditions and find new opportunities.
4. The frontier played a key role in stimulating American nationalism and individualism.
5. Because of the frontier, America did not have a hereditary landed aristocracy.

Test Tip

What first comes to your mind when you think of the Old West? Most Americans probably think of Custer's Last Stand, Chief Sitting Bull, cattle drives, and gun duels between lawmen and outlaws. As you might guess, APUSH test writers have a very different set of priorities. Although it is unlikely that your exam will have questions about Custer and Sitting Bull, there is a high probability that you will have to identify Helen Hunt Jackson's book Century of Dishonor *and Frederick Jackson Turner's frontier thesis.*

INDUSTRIAL AMERICA
———1865–1900

I. BIG BUSINESS

A. THE CONSOLIDATION OF BIG BUSINESS

1. Vertical integration occurs when a company controls both the production and distribution of its product. For example, Andrew Carnegie used vertical integration to gain control over the U.S. steel industry.

2. Horizontal integration occurs when one company gains control over other companies that produce the same product.

3. By the end of the nineteenth century, monopolies and trusts exercised a significant degree of control over key aspects of the American economy.

B. CONSEQUENCES OF CONSOLIDATION

1. Corporations built large, systematically organized factories where work was increasingly performed by machines and unskilled workers.

2. Corporations introduced systems of "scientific management," also known as Taylorism, to increase factory production and lower labor costs.

3. Corporations accumulated vast sums of investment capital.

4. Corporations used the railroads to help develop national markets for their goods.

C. CELEBRATING AMERICA'S INDUSTRIAL SUCCESS

1. The World's Columbian Exposition of 1893 showcased America's industrial development.
2. The popular Horatio Alger Jr. stories provided concrete examples of the ideal of the self-made man.

II. LABOR AND LABOR UNIONS, 1865–1900

A. KEY TRENDS

1. Immigrants, women, and children significantly expanded the labor force.
2. Machines increasingly replaced skilled artisans.
3. Large bureaucratic corporations dominated the American economy.
4. Corporations developed national and even international markets for their goods.

B. THE KNIGHTS OF LABOR

1. The Knights were led by Terence V. Powderly. Under his leadership, the Knights grew rapidly, peaking at 730,000 members in 1886.
2. The Knights grew rapidly because of their open-membership policy, the continuing industrialization of the American economy, and the growth of urban population.
3. The Knights welcomed unskilled and semiskilled workers, including women, immigrants, and African Americans.
4. The Knights were idealists who believed they could eliminate conflict between labor and management. Their goal was to create a cooperative society in which laborers, not capitalists, owned the industries in which they worked.
5. The Haymarket Square riot was unfairly blamed on the Knights. As a result, the public associated them with anarchists.

C. THE INDUSTRIAL WORKERS OF THE WORLD

1. The Industrial Workers of the World (IWW) was led by "Mother" Jones, Elizabeth Flynn, and Big Bill Haywood.

2. Like the Knights of Labor, the IWW strove to unite all laborers, including unskilled African Americans, who were excluded from craft unions.

3. The IWW's motto was "An injury to one is an injury to all," and its goal was to create "One Big Union."

4. Unlike the Knights, the IWW (or Wobblies) embraced the rhetoric of class conflict and endorsed violent tactics.

5. IWW membership probably never exceeded 150,000 workers. The organization collapsed during World War I.

D. THE AMERICAN FEDERATION OF LABOR

1. The American Federation of Labor (AFL) was led by Samuel Gompers, the leader of the Cigar Makers Union.

2. The AFL was an alliance of skilled workers in craft unions.

3. Under Gompers' leadership, the AFL concentrated on bread-and-butter issues such as higher wages, shorter hours, and better working conditions.

It is very important to understand the similarities and differences among the Knights of Labor, Industrial Workers of the World, and the American Federation of Labor. All three were dedicated to organizing laborers. The Knights and the IWW both attempted to organize all skilled and unskilled workers into one union. However, the Knights strove for a cooperative society, while the IWW embraced class conflict and violent tactics. In contrast, the AFL organized skilled workers, repudiated violence, and fought for higher wages and better working conditions.

E. THE PULLMAN STRIKE, 1894

1. During the late nineteenth century, the American labor movement experienced a number of violent strikes. The two best-known strikes were the Homestead Strike (1892) and the Pullman Strike (1894).

2. When the national economy fell into a depression, the Pullman Palace Car Company cut wages while maintaining rents and prices in a company town where 12,000 workers lived. This action precipitated the Pullman Strike.

3. The Pullman Strike halted a substantial portion of American railroad commerce.

4. The strike ended when President Cleveland ordered federal troops to Chicago, ostensibly to protect rail-carried mail but, in reality, to crush the strike.

III. IMMIGRATION

A. THE NEW IMMIGRANTS

1. Prior to 1880, most immigrants to the United States came from the British Isles and Western Europe.
2. Beginning in the 1880s, a new wave of immigrants left Europe for America. The so-called New Immigrants came from small towns and villages in southern and eastern Europe. The majority lived in Italy, Russia, Poland, and Austria-Hungary.
3. The New Immigrants primarily settled in large cities in the Northeast and Midwest.
4. Very few New Immigrants settled in the South.

B. THE CHINESE EXCLUSION ACT OF 1882

1. This was the first law in American history to exclude a group from America because of ethnic background.
2. The act prohibited the immigration of Chinese to America.
3. Working-class Americans who felt threatened by Chinese workers strongly supported the law.
4. Support for the law was particularly strong in California.

C. NATIVIST OPPOSITION TO THE NEW IMMIGRANTS

1. Nativists had previously opposed Irish and German Catholic immigrants.
2. Nativists opposed the New Immigrants for the following reasons:
   - *The immigrants were heavily Catholic and Jewish.*
   - *They spoke different languages and practiced different cultural traditions.*
   - *They did not understand American political traditions.*
   - *They threatened to take away jobs because they were willing to work for low wages.*

IV. THE NEW INDUSTRIAL ORDER: SUPPORTERS AND REFORMERS

A. SOCIAL DARWINISM

1. Social Darwinism is the belief that the fittest survive in both nature and society.
2. Wealthy business and industrial leaders used Social Darwinism to justify their success.
3. Social Darwinists believed that industrial and urban problems are part of a natural evolutionary process that humans cannot control.

B. GOSPEL OF WEALTH

1. This gospel was promoted by Andrew Carnegie.
2. It expressed the belief that, as the guardians of society's wealth, the rich have a duty to serve society.
3. Over his lifetime, Carnegie donated more than $350 million to support libraries, school, peace initiatives, and the arts.

C. SOCIAL GOSPEL

1. The Social Gospel was a reform movement based on the belief that Christians have a responsibility to confront social problems.
2. Christian ministers were among the leaders of the Social Gospel movement.

V. LITERARY AND ARTISTIC MOVEMENTS

A. LITERATURE

1. Realism was the most significant movement in American literature during the late nineteenth century.
2. Edward Bellamy's book *Looking Backward: 2000 to 1887* was a utopian reaction to the author's disillusionment with the problems created by the growth of industrialism.

B. ART

1. The Ashcan School of art focused on urban scenes such as crowded tenements and boisterous barrooms.

2. The 1913 International Exhibition of Modern Art (or Armory Show) provided the American public's first exposure to the new trends in European art. Astonished visitors saw Cubism and other forms of modern art. The show served as a catalyst for American artists, who began to experiment with the new styles.

POPULISM AND PROGRESSIVISM
1890–1917

 I. AGRARIAN DISCONTENT

A. CAUSES OF AGRARIAN DISCONTENT

1. Belief that railroads were using discriminatory rates to exploit farmers
2. Belief that big business used high tariffs to exploit farmers
3. Belief that a deflationary monetary policy based on gold hurt farmers
4. Belief that corporations charged exorbitant prices for fertilizers and farm machinery

B. THE POPULIST OR PEOPLE'S PARTY

1. The Populist Party attempted to unite discontented farmers.
2. It attempted to improve their economic conditions.
3. It attempted to support the following:
   - *Increasing the money supply with the free and unlimited coinage of silver and gold at the legal ratio of 16 to 1*
   - *Using the Interstate Commerce Act of 1887 to regulate railroads and prevent discrimination against small customers*
   - *Organizing cooperative marketing societies*
   - *Supporting the candidacy of William Jennings Bryan in the 1896 presidential election*

C. REASONS THE POPULIST PARTY FAILED

1. Western and Southern farmers did not agree on political strategies.
2. Racism prevented poor White and Black farmers from working together.
3. The dramatic increases in urban population caused by the wave of New Immigrants led to higher prices for agricultural products.
4. The discovery of gold in the Yukon increased the supply of gold, thus easing farmers' access to credit.
5. The Democratic Party absorbed many Populist programs.
6. William Jennings Bryan lost the 1896 presidential election to William McKinley and the Republicans.

II. THE PROGRESSIVES

A. KEY POINTS

1. Progressive leaders were primarily middle-class reformers concerned with urban and consumer issues.
2. Progressive reformers believed that government should be used to ameliorate social problems.
3. Progressive reformers wanted to use governmental power to regulate industrial production and improve labor conditions.
4. Progressive reformers rejected Social Darwinism, arguing that cooperation offered the best way to improve society.

B. KEY GOALS

1. Democratization of the political process
   ▸ *Direct election of senators*
   ▸ *Women's suffrage*
2. Reform of local governments
   ▸ *Initiative, recall, and referendum—ways to make local governments more responsive to public opinion*
   ▸ *Commission or city-manager forms of government to make local governments more professional*
   ▸ *Nonpartisan local governments to weaken political machines*

3. Regulation of big business
   ▸ *Passage of child labor laws*
   ▸ *Passage of antitrust legislation*
   ▸ *Passage of Pure Food and Drug Act*

Test Tip

It is important to remember what the Progressives fought for. It is also important to remember what they did not fight for. Progressives did not fight for the passage of civil rights laws or the creation of a socialist commonwealth.

C. PROGRESSIVE CONSTITUTIONAL AMENDMENTS

1. The Sixteenth Amendment gave Congress the power to lay and collect income taxes.
2. The Seventeenth Amendment provided that senators shall be elected by popular vote.
3. The Eighteenth Amendment forbade the sale or manufacture of intoxicating liquors.
4. The Nineteenth Amendment granted women the right to vote.

III. THE MUCKRAKERS

A. KEY POINTS

1. Muckrakers were investigative reporters who promoted social and political reforms by exposing corruption and urban problems.
2. Muckrakers were the leading critics of urban bosses and corporate robber barons.
3. The rise of mass-circulation newspapers and magazines enabled muckrakers to reach a large audience.

B. LEADING MUCKRAKERS

1. Upton Sinclair
   ▸ *Sinclair wrote the novel* The Jungle, *graphically exposing abuses in the meatpacking industry.*
   ▸ *He helped convince Congress to pass the Meat Inspection Act of 1906 and the Pure Food and Drug Act.*

CHRONOLOGICAL REVIEW

2. Jacob Riis
   ▸ *Riis was a journalist and photographer working primarily in New York City.*
   ▸ *Riis's book* How the Other Half Lives *provided poignant pictures that gave a human face to the poverty and despair experienced by immigrants living in New York City's Lower East Side.*

3. Ida Tarbell
   ▸ *Tarbell was the foremost woman in the muckraking movement.*
   ▸ *She published a highly critical history of the Standard Oil Company, calling it the* Mother of Trusts.

Most APUSH students can identify Upton Sinclair and Ida Tarbell. However, few can identify Jacob Riis. APUSH test writers are aware of this inconsistency and have devoted a number of questions to Riis and his work.

IV. THE PROGRESSIVE PRESIDENTS

A. THEODORE ROOSEVELT

1. Teddy Roosevelt addressed all of the following Progressive issues:
   ▸ *Conservation of natural resources and wildlife*
   ▸ *Unsanitary conditions in the meatpacking industry*
   ▸ *Monopolization and consolidation in the railroad industry*
   ▸ *Unsafe drug products*

2. He promoted a Square Deal for labor by using arbitration to settle the Anthracite Coal Strike of 1902.

3. Roosevelt ran as the Progressive or Bull Moose candidate for President in the 1912 presidential election.

B. WOODROW WILSON

1. Wilson was a vigorous reformer who launched an all-out assault on high tariffs, banking problems, and the trusts.

2. Wilson supported the Federal Reserve Act of 1913. The landmark act established a system of district banks coordinated by a central board. The new Federal Reserve system made currency and credit more elastic.

Test Tip

Theodore Roosevelt, William Taft, and Woodrow Wilson all supported Progressive reforms. However, they do not receive equal treatment on APUSH exams. Test writers focus almost all of their attention on Teddy Roosevelt, while omitting Taft and limiting questions on Wilson to the Federal Reserve Act. As you will see in Chapter 14, there are a number of questions about Wilson's foreign policy.

V. REFORMERS AND SUFFRAGETTES, 1865–1920

A. JANE ADDAMS

1. Jane Addams is best known for founding Hull House in Chicago.
2. Hull House and other settlement houses were dedicated to helping the urban poor.
3. Settlement-house workers established day nurseries for working mothers, published reports condemning deplorable housing conditions, and taught literacy classes.

B. THE FIGHT FOR SUFFRAGE

1. Frontier life tended to promote the acceptance of greater equality for women.
2. The only states with complete women's suffrage before 1900 were located west of the Mississippi. Wyoming (1869) was the first state to grant women the full right to vote.
3. The Nineteenth Amendment (1920) guaranteed women the right to vote.

C. THE WOMEN'S CHRISTIAN TEMPERANCE UNION (WCTU)

1. Carry Nation was one of the best known and most outspoken leaders of the WCTU.
2. The WCTU successfully convinced many women that they had a moral responsibility to improve society by working for prohibition.

D. WOMEN AND THE PROGRESSIVE REFORMS

1. Dorothea Dix worked tirelessly on behalf of the mentally ill.

2. Ida B. Wells-Barnett was an African American civil rights advocate and an early women's rights advocate. She is noted for her opposition to lynching.

3. Women reformers were also actively involved in the following Progressive Era reforms:

   ▸ *Passage of child labor legislation at the state level*

   ▸ *Campaigns to limit the working hours of women and children*

E. WOMEN AND THE WORKPLACE

1. During the late nineteenth and early twentieth centuries, the majority of female workers employed outside the home were young and unmarried.

2. During the late nineteenth and early twentieth centuries, women were most likely to work outside their homes as one of the following:

   ▸ *Domestic servants*

   ▸ *Garment workers*

   ▸ *Teachers*

   ▸ *Cigar makers*

3. During the late nineteenth century, women were least likely to work outside their homes as either of these:

   ▸ *Physicians*

   ▸ *Lawyers*

VI. BLACK AMERICANS DURING THE PROGRESSIVE ERA, 1897–1917

A. W.E.B. DU BOIS

1. During the Progressive Era, W.E.B. Du Bois emerged as the most influential advocate of full political, economic, and social equality for Black Americans.

2. Du Bois founded the National Association for the Advancement of Colored People (NAACP) in 1909.

3. Du Bois advocated the intellectual development of a "talented tenth" of the Black population. Du Bois hoped that the talented tenth would become influential by, for example, continuing their education, writing books, or becoming directly involved in social change.

4. Du Bois opposed the implementation of Booker T. Washington's program for Black progress. Du Bois supported cooperation with White people to further Black progress. His goal was integration, not Black separatism.

B. THE NAACP

1. The NAACP rejected Booker T. Washington's gradualism and separatism.

2. The NAACP focused on using the courts to achieve equality and justice.

C. *THE BIRTH OF A NATION* AND THE RESURGENCE OF THE KKK

1. The KKK first emerged during Radical Reconstruction (1865–1877)

2. D. W. Griffith's epic film *The Birth of a Nation* (1915) became controversial because of its depiction of KKK activities as heroic and commendable.

3. *The Birth of a Nation* played a role in the resurgence of the KKK during the Progressive Era.

4. The KKK favored White supremacy and immigration restriction.

IMPERIALISM AND WORLD WAR I
1890–1919

I. AMERICAN IMPERIALISM: POLITICAL AND ECONOMIC EXPANSION

A. GENERAL CAUSES OF AMERICAN IMPERIALISM

1. The sensational stories published by "yellow journalists"
2. The New Navy policy promoted by Alfred Thayer Mahan and Theodore Roosevelt
3. The example of European imperialism in Africa
4. The emphasis of Social Darwinism on survival of the fittest
5. Unlike Manifest Destiny, imperialism included the idea of moral improvement by bringing the blessings of civilization to less technologically advanced people.

B. SPANISH-AMERICAN WAR

1. Causes
   ▸ *The battleship* Maine *was sunk mysteriously in Havana harbor.*
   ▸ *A circulation battle between the "yellow journalism" newspapers of Joseph Pulitzer and William Randolph Hearst. Their sensational headlines and lurid stories aroused public support for a war to liberate Cuba from Spanish control.*
2. Territorial Acquisitions
   ▸ *As a result of the Spanish-American War, Spain relinquished control of Puerto Rico, Cuba, Guam, and the Philippines to the United States.*
   ▸ *By establishing a protectorate over Cuba, the United States began implementing an imperialist foreign policy.*

3. The Debate Over Annexing the Philippines
   ▸ *The Anti-Imperialism League opposed annexation, arguing that it violated America's long-established commitment to the principles of self-determination and anti-colonialism.*
   ▸ *Supporters of annexation argued that America had a moral responsibility to "civilize" the islands. They also pointed out that the Philippines could become a valuable trading partner.*

C. THE ROOSEVELT COROLLARY TO THE MONROE DOCTRINE, 1904

1. President Theodore Roosevelt worried that the Dominican Republic and other Latin American nations would default on debts owed to European banks. These defaults could then provoke European military intervention.
2. Roosevelt issued the Roosevelt Corollary to the Monroe Doctrine to forestall European intervention.
3. The Roosevelt Corollary expanded America's role in Central America and the Caribbean.
4. The Roosevelt Corollary claimed America's right to assume the role of "an international police power." Presidents Roosevelt, Taft, and Wilson enforced the Roosevelt Corollary by sending American troops to Cuba, Panama, Nicaragua, the Dominican Republic, Mexico, and Haiti.
5. Theodore Roosevelt explained and justified the Roosevelt Corollary as follows:

   "Chronic wrongdoing, or an impotence which results in a general loosening of the ties of civilized society, may in America, as elsewhere, ultimately require intervention by some civilized nation, and in the Western Hemisphere the adherence of the United States to the Monroe Doctrine may force the United States . . . to the exercise of an international police power."

D. TAFT AND DOLLAR DIPLOMACY

1. President Taft believed he could use economic investments to bolster American foreign policy.
2. Taft's attempt to use Dollar Diplomacy in Asia and Latin America achieved very little success.

E. THE OPEN DOOR POLICY

1. As China's Qing (Manchu) dynasty weakened, European powers carved out spheres of influence where they exercised political leverage and obtained exclusive commercial privileges.

2. Although he knew he could not force the Europeans to leave China, Secretary of State John Hay was determined to protect American missionaries and commercial interests.

3. In 1899, Hay sent the nations with spheres of influence in China a note calling for open access to China for American investment and commercial interests.

4. Known as the Open Door, the policy underscored America's commitment to free trade and opposition to obstacles that thwarted international commerce.

> *The Open Door policy is easy to overlook. Most APUSH textbooks devote less than a page to the topic. Don't be deceived by this modest coverage. The Open Door has a high priority in the minds of APUSH test writers. The Open Door has been on all but one of the released exams. Be sure you know that the Open Door was intended to protect American commercial interests in China.*

II. THE ROAD TO WAR

A. AMERICAN NEUTRALITY

1. President Wilson sought to distance America from World War I by issuing a proclamation of neutrality.

2. Wilson's policy of neutrality was consistent with America's traditional policy of avoiding European entanglements.

3. Wilson insisted that all belligerents respect American neutral rights on the high seas.

B. THE GERMAN CHALLENGE TO AMERICAN NEUTRALITY

1. Faced with a stalemate in the trenches across France and a British blockade that was exhausting its ability to continue fighting, Germany launched a campaign of unrestricted submarine warfare in early February 1917.

2. In late February 1917, the German foreign secretary, Arthur Zimmerman, sent a secret telegram to the German minister in Mexico. Intercepted by British intelligence, the telegram asked Mexico to join a military alliance against the United States. In return, the Germans promised to help Mexico recover territories it had lost following the Mexican War.

C. WILSON'S WAR MESSAGE

1. Wilson accused the Germans of violating freedom of the seas, killing innocent Americans, and interfering with Mexico.
2. Wilson galvanized public opinion by calling on America to launch a noble crusade "to make the world safe for democracy."

III. WORLD WAR I AT HOME AND ABROAD

A. THE BLACK MIGRATION

1. Causes of the migration:
   ▶ *Jim Crow laws denied African Americans their rights as citizens and forced them to endure poverty and systematic discrimination.*
   ▶ *Beginning with World War I, the wartime demand for labor attracted African Americans to cities in the North and West.*
2. Exodus from the rural South:
   ▶ *In 1915, the overwhelming majority of African Americans lived in the rural South.*
   ▶ *Attracted by the wartime demand for labor, African Americans migrated to urban centers in the North and West.*

B. THE COMMITTEE ON PUBLIC INFORMATION

1. The Committee on Public Information used propaganda to arouse public support for the war and stifle dissent.
2. Americans were persuaded to buy war bonds and believe that Germany was a particularly barbarous nation.

IV. TREATY OF VERSAILLES

A. THE FOURTEEN POINTS

1. Wilson's Fourteen Points included a call for the following:
   ▶ *Open diplomacy*
   ▶ *Freedom of the seas*
   ▶ *The creation of an international organization to preserve the peace and security of its members*
   ▶ *National self-determination for oppressed minority groups*
2. Wilson's Fourteen Points did not include the following:
   ▶ *Recognition of Allied economic and territorial agreements made during the war*
   ▶ *A provision to create the International Monetary Fund*

B. REASONS THE UNITED STATES DID NOT JOIN THE LEAGUE OF NATIONS

1. Wilson refused to compromise on the issue of America's unconditional adherence to the charter of the League of Nations. This hardened Senate opposition to the Treaty of Versailles.
2. Opponents believed that the League would lead to further involvement in foreign wars.
3. Senator Lodge was a skillful opponent of the League. The personal and political rivalry between Wilson and Lodge precluded any chance of a compromise.

V. THE "RED SCARE" OF 1919–1920

A. THE BOLSHEVIK REVOLUTION IN RUSSIA

1. Led by Lenin, the Bolsheviks overthrew the czar and seized power in Russia.
2. Widespread postwar labor strikes confused and frightened Americans.

B. THE PALMER RAIDS OF 1919–1920

1. The Palmer Raids were caused by the fear of communism and radicalism.

2. These raids were conducted against suspected communists and anarchists.

3. The Palmer Raids disregarded basic civil liberties. For example, government agents in 33 cities broke into meeting halls and homes without search warrants. More than 4,000 people were jailed and denied counsel.

THE
ROARING TWENTIES

I. ECONOMIC CONDITIONS

A. SIGNS OF PROSPERITY

1. During the 1920s, the standard of living rose, and more and more people moved to urban centers.
2. All of the following provided evidence of economic prosperity during the 1920s:
   ▶ *Larger numbers of women and men working in office jobs*
   ▶ *Increased emphasis on the marketing of consumer goods*
   ▶ *Growing investment in the stock market*
3. The assembly-line production of Henry Ford's Model T enabled average American families to purchase automobiles.
4. Beginning in 1920, the number of children aged ten to fifteen who were in the industrial workforce began to decline.

B. SIGNS OF TROUBLE

1. The least-prosperous group in the 1920s consisted of farmers in the Midwest and South.
2. For American farmers, the years 1921 to 1929 were a period of falling prices for agricultural products.

II. REPUBLICAN POLITICS: HARDING, COOLIDGE, AND HOOVER

A. REPUBLICAN PROSPERITY

1. Republican presidents of the 1920s favored tax cuts for wealthy Americans.
2. During the presidencies of Harding and Coolidge, the federal agencies created during the Progressive Era aided business.

B. FOREIGN POLICY

1. Despite its isolationist position in the 1920s, the U.S. government actively participated in decisions regarding international finance and the payment of war reparations.
2. The Kellogg-Briand Pact of 1928 was an international agreement in which 62 nations pledged to foreswear war as an instrument of policy.
3. The Washington Naval Conference of 1921–1922 was called to restrain the naval arms race among the United States, Britain, Japan, Italy, and France. The signatory nations agreed to specific limitations on the number of battleships each nation could build.
4. The United States responded to the economic crisis in Germany during the 1920s by adopting the Dawes Plan. The plan rescheduled German reparation payments and opened the way for American private loans to Germany.

III. THE CULTURE OF MODERNISM: THE ARTS AND MASS ENTERTAINMENT

A. THE ARTS

1. The "Lost Generation of the 1920s"
   ▸ *Key writers included Sinclair Lewis and F. Scott Fitzgerald.*
   ▸ *They were called the Lost Generation because they were disillusioned with American society during the 1920s.*
   ▸ *Writers criticized middle-class materialism and conformity. For example, Sinclair Lewis criticized middle-class life in novels such as* Babbitt *and* Main Street.

> *Recall that according to the APUSH rubric (see Chapter 1), 40 percent of the multiple-choice questions cover social change and cultural and intellectual developments. Given this requirement, the "Lost Generation" of writers is a favorite topic for APUSH test writers. The key point to remember is that writers such as F. Scott Fitzgerald and Sinclair Lewis criticized middle-class materialism and conformity.*

2. Jazz

> ▸ *Black musicians such as Joseph ("Joe") King Oliver, W. C. Handy, and "Jelly Roll" Morton helped create jazz.*
> ▸ *Jazz was especially popular among the youth because it symbolized a desire to break with tradition.*

B. MASS ENTERTAINMENT

1. Movies were the most popular form of mass entertainment.
2. Led by baseball, sports became a big business.
3. During the 1920s, technological innovations made long-distance radio broadcasting possible. National radio networks reached millions of Americans.

IV. RESPONSES TO MODERNISM: RELIGIOUS FUNDAMENTALISM AND NATIVISM

A. RELIGIOUS FUNDAMENTALISM

1. Fundamentalism was an anti-liberal and anti-secular movement that gained strength throughout the 1920s.
2. The Scopes Trial was an important test case.

> ▸ *John T. Scopes was a high school biology teacher in Tennessee who was indicted for teaching evolution.*
> ▸ *The Scopes Trial illustrates the cultural conflict in the 1920s between fundamentalism and modernism.*

B. NATIVISM

1. The Ku Klux Klan (KKK)

> ▸ *The 1920s witnessed a dramatic expansion of the KKK.*
> ▸ *D. W. Griffith's full-length film* The Birth of a Nation *glorified the KKK.*

▶ *During the 1920s, the KKK favored White supremacy and restrictions on immigration.*

▶ *The KKK was hostile toward immigrants, Catholics, Jews, and African Americans.*

Test Tip

Although the KKK is a particularly distasteful topic, don't skip it. The resurgence of the Klan during the 1920s provides a good example of the nativist reaction to modernism. Also be sure you can identify D. W. Griffith's film **The Birth of a Nation.**

2. The National Origins Act of 1924

▶ *The primary purpose of the National Origins Act was to use quotas to restrict the flow of newcomers from Southern and Eastern Europe.*

▶ *The quotas established by the National Origins Act discriminated against immigrants from Southern and Eastern Europe. These quotas were the primary reason for the decrease in the numbers of Europeans immigrating to the United States in the 1920s.*

▶ *The number of Mexicans and Puerto Ricans migrating to the United States increased because neither group was affected by the restrictive immigration acts of 1921 and 1924.*

3. The Sacco and Vanzetti Case

▶ *The Sacco and Vanzetti case was significant because it illustrated a fear of radicals and recent immigrants.*

V. THE STRUGGLE FOR EQUALITY: AFRICAN AMERICANS AND WOMEN

A. AFRICAN AMERICANS

1. The Harlem Renaissance

▶ *The Harlem Renaissance thrived during the 1920s.*

▶ *The Harlem Renaissance was an outpouring of Black artistic and literary creativity.*

▶ *Harlem Renaissance writers and artists expressed pride in their African American culture. They supported full social and political equality for African Americans.*

▸ *Key figures in the Harlem Renaissance included James Weldon Johnson, Zora Neale Hurston, Langston Hughes, and Josephine Baker.*

2. The Great Migration

▸ *The migration of Black Americans from the rural South to the urban North and West continued during the 1920s.*

▸ *The demand for industrial workers was the primary pull; the primary push came from the restrictions of Jim Crow segregation.*

3. Marcus Garvey

▸ *Marcus Garvey was the charismatic leader of the Universal Negro Improvement Association.*

▸ *Garveyism was identified with the following:*
      Black pride
      Black economic development
      Black nationalism
      Pan-Africanism

▸ *Garvey was committed to the idea that Black Americans should return to Africa.*

B. WOMEN

1. Flappers

▸ *Flappers symbolized the new freedom by challenging traditional American attitudes about women.*

▸ *Flappers favored short bobbed hair, smoked cigarettes, and even wore the new one-piece bathing suits.*

2. Women and the Workforce

▸ *Although new jobs became available in offices and stores, the percentage of single women in the labor force actually declined between 1920 and 1930.*

▸ *Women did not receive equal pay and continued to face discrimination in the professions.*

▸ *Most married women did not seek employment outside the home.*

3. Margaret Sanger

▸ *Margaret Sanger was an outspoken reformer who openly championed birth control for women.*

4. Factors causing the decline of the feminist movement during the 1920s:

   ▸ *Passage of the Nineteenth Amendment granting women the right to vote*
   ▸ *The inability of women's groups to agree on goals*
   ▸ *The decline of the Progressive reform movement*

THE

GREAT DEPRESSION

AND THE NEW DEAL

1929–1941

I. CAUSES OF THE GREAT DEPRESSION

A. CONSEQUENCES OF THE 1929 STOCK MARKET CRASH

1. A loss of confidence in the stock market
2. A reduction in the output of manufactured goods
3. A decline in investment in capital goods

B. OVERPRODUCTION AND UNDERCONSUMPTION

1. Companies overproduced consumer goods.
2. Consumers did not have enough money or credit to purchase goods.

C. DECLINE IN FARM PROSPERITY

1. The decline in farm prosperity in the 1920s was an important factor contributing to the Great Depression in the 1930s.
2. Depression of the prices of agricultural products during the 1920s was an important sign of economic weakness.

D. INTERNATIONAL TRADE

1. Serious dislocations in international trade were a significant cause of the Great Depression.
2. The Hawley-Smoot Tariff Act of 1930 raised tariffs, thus triggering a decline in trade. Within three years, world trade declined in value by 40 percent.

II. HERBERT HOOVER AND THE GREAT DEPRESSION

A. THE BONUS EXPEDITIONARY FORCE

1. In 1932, a ragtag "army" of World War I veterans known as the Bonus Expeditionary Force marched on Washington, D.C. Their objective was to demand that Congress pay them a bonus, which had been promised to World War I veterans.
2. President Hoover used force to disband the Bonus Expeditionary Force.

B. HOOVER'S ECONOMIC POLICIES

1. President Hoover believed that the economic recovery of the United States depended primarily on the business community.
2. President Hoover approached the task of caring for unemployed workers by emphasizing the importance of private charities.
3. President Hoover supported federal loans to private businesses and to state and local governments.
4. President Hoover established the Reconstruction Finance Corporation (RFC) in a belated attempt to fight the Great Depression.

III. FRANKLIN D. ROOSEVELT AND THE NEW DEAL

A. GOALS

1. The three Rs were Relief, Recovery, and Reform.
2. Unlike Hoover, FDR favored direct federal relief to individuals.
3. The New Deal was a reform program that sought to restructure American capitalism rather than replace it with a socialist system.
4. The program used deficit spending on public works programs to revive the economy.

B. THE FIRST HUNDRED DAYS

1. All of the following concerns were addressed during the First Hundred Days of the New Deal:

▸ *Restoring public confidence in the banking system
(Note: The New Deal did not propose legislation that
would nationalize the banks.)*

▸ *Creating new jobs in the public sector to reduce
unemployment*

▸ *Raising farm prices by restricting agricultural production*

▸ *Providing mortgage support for homeowners*

▸ *Creating the Tennessee Valley Authority as a model
project to provide cheap electricity, prevent floods, and
serve as an experiment in regional planning*

2. All of the following were passed during the First Hundred Days:
   ▸ *The Civilian Conservation Corps*
   ▸ *The National Recovery Administration*
   ▸ *The Agricultural Adjustment Act*
   ▸ *The Tennessee Valley Authority*

C. FARM POLICY: THE AGRICULTURAL ADJUSTMENT ACT (AAA) OF 1933

1. The purpose of the Agricultural Adjustment Act (AAA)
   of 1933 was to raise farm prices by limiting agricultural
   production.

2. The AAA established a national system of crop controls
   and offered subsidies to farmers who agreed to limit the
   production of specific crops.

3. Although the AAA was based on sound economic principles,
   it seemed to defy common sense. Hungry Americans were
   outraged when farmers plowed crops under and destroyed
   millions of piglets.

D. THE NATIONAL INDUSTRIAL RECOVERY ACT (NRA)

1. The National Industrial Recovery Act (NRA) sought to combat
   the Great Depression by fostering government–business
   cooperation.

2. The NRA allowed businesses to regulate themselves through
   codes of fair competition.

3. The NRA did not succeed. In contrast, Social Security proved
   to be much more enduring.

E. THE CIVILIAN CONSERVATION CORPS

1. The CCC was created during the First Hundred Days of the New Deal.
2. It established a jobs program for unemployed youth.

F. THE SOCIAL SECURITY ACT OF 1935

1. The Social Security Act created a federal pension system funded by taxes on a worker's wages and by an equivalent contribution by employers.
2. The aging of the U.S. population is now widely seen as a threat to the long-term viability of the Social Security system.

G. THE WAGNER ACT OF 1935

1. The Wagner Act is also known as the National Labor Relations Act.
2. It is often called the Magna Carta of labor because it ensured workers' right to organize and bargain collectively.
3. It led to a dramatic increase in labor union membership.

H. THE NEW DEAL AND BLACK AMERICANS

1. New Deal programs helped Black Americans survive some of the worst hardships of the Great Depression.
2. The New Deal did not directly confront racial segregation and injustice. As a result, there was no major action on civil rights.

I. THE COURT-PACKING SCHEME

1. Much to FDR's chagrin, the Supreme Court declared key parts of the New Deal unconstitutional.
2. FDR responded by attempting to "pack" (add more justices to) the Supreme Court. His goal was to make sure that New Deal laws would be found constitutional.

J. IMPACT OF THE NEW DEAL

1. Historians generally regard the New Deal as a program of reform rather than of revolution because the New Deal sought to restructure American capitalism rather than replace it.

2. The New Deal did mark a new direction for the federal government. For example, New Deal programs all demonstrated a willingness to use the government to enhance social welfare.

3. The New Deal programs were partially successful in reducing unemployment and reviving the economy.

4. The New Deal led to the emergence of the Democratic Party as the majority party.

5. The New Deal helped African Americans survive the Great Depression. (*Note*: New Deal programs did *not* directly confront racial injustice.)

6. It is important to remember that the United States did not fully emerge from the Great Depression until the massive military expenditures prompted by World War II.

7. Key things that the New Deal did *not* do include the following:

   ▸ *The New Deal did* not *integrate the armed forces.*

   ▸ *The New Deal did* not *sponsor the Equal Rights Amendment.*

   ▸ *The New Deal did* not *include programs specifically designed to protect the civil liberties of African Americans.*

   ▸ *The New Deal did* not *establish the Bureau of Indian Affairs.*

   ▸ *The New Deal did* not *nationalize basic industries.*

   ▸ *The New Deal did* not *provide for legal recognition of unions for migrant workers.*

It is very important to remember New Deal programs and accomplishments. It is equally important to know what programs and accomplishments were not *part of the New Deal. APUSH test writers construct a number of questions asking you to identify programs that were* not *part of the New Deal. Be sure to carefully study the list of programs that were* not *part of the New Deal.*

IV. LABOR AND UNION RECOGNITION

A. THE CIO AND JOHN L. LEWIS

1. The CIO (Congress of Industrial Organizations) organized unskilled and semiskilled factory workers in basic manufacturing industries such as steel and automobiles.

2. Here is how John L. Lewis explained the goals and strategy of the CIO:

   "The productive methods and facilities of modern industry have been completely transformed. . . . Skilled artisans make up only a small proportion of the workers. Obviously the bargaining strength of employees under these conditions no longer rests in organizations of skilled craftsmen. It is dependent upon a national union representing all employees—whether skilled or unskilled, or whether working by brain or brawn—in each basic industry."

B. THE SPLIT BETWEEN THE AFL AND THE CIO

1. The American Federation of Labor (AFL) split apart at its national convention in 1935.

2. A majority of AFL leaders refused to grant charters to new unions that were organized on an industry-wide basis.

3. The AFL favored the organization of workers according to their skills and trades.

4. The CIO favored the organization of all workers in a particular industry.

V. THE NEW DEAL COALITION

A. THE DEMOCRATIC COALITION

1. All of the following were part of the Democratic Coalition that elected FDR in 1936:

   ▶ *White Southerners*

   ▶ *African Americans*

   ▶ *Ethnic minorities*

   ▶ *Union members*

2. The Democratic Coalition did *not* include wealthy industrialists.

B. SHIFT IN VOTING

1. As a result of the Emancipation Proclamation and the Reconstruction amendments, African Americans were loyal voters for the Republican Party.
2. During the presidency of Franklin D. Roosevelt, large numbers of Black voters switched their allegiance from the Republican Party to the Democratic Party.

> *Although the New Deal was popular, it did have a number of outspoken critics. For example, Dr. Francis E. Townsend, Gerald Smith, Huey Long, and Father Charles Coughlin all criticized aspects of the New Deal.*

VI. AMERICAN SOCIETY DURING THE NEW DEAL

A. HOOVERVILLES

1. Millions of Americans were evicted from their homes and apartments because they could not pay their mortgage or rent.
2. Hoovervilles (shantytowns of unemployed and homeless people) sprang up in most American cities.

B. PEOPLE ON THE MOVE

1. During the 1930s, the Great Depression led to a mass migration of Americans looking for work.
2. African Americans continued to migrate from small Southern towns to urban centers in the North and West.

WORLD WAR II
1941–1945

I. **AMERICAN RESPONSES TO THE GROWING THREAT OF WAR**

A. THE STIMSON DOCTRINE, 1932

1. In September 1931, the Japanese invaded and conquered the Chinese province of Manchuria.

2. Proclaimed in 1932, the Stimson Doctrine declared that the United States would not recognize any territorial acquisitions achieved by force. Although the United States did not recognize the Japanese occupation, the Hoover administration refrained from taking any military action.

3. The failure of the United States and other powers to take any concrete action marked the failure of collective security.

B. THE NEUTRALITY ACTS

1. The Neutrality Acts of the 1930s were expressions of a commitment to isolationism.

2. During the 1930s, isolationists drew support for their position from Washington's Farewell Address.

C. THE LEND-LEASE PROGRAM

1. Under the Lend-Lease program, President Roosevelt authorized the sale of surplus military equipment to the Allies.

2. The Lend-Lease program was used primarily to help Great Britain and the Soviet Union resist Nazi Germany.

II. THE ATTACK ON PEARL HARBOR AND THE GERMANY-FIRST STRATEGY

A. PEARL HARBOR

1. The Japanese war machine was dependent on shipments of oil, aviation gasoline, steel, and scrap iron from the United States. In late 1940, the Roosevelt administration imposed the first of a series of embargoes on Japan-bound supplies. In mid-1941, President Franklin D. Roosevelt froze Japanese assets in the United States and halted all shipments of gasoline.

2. The U.S. actions left Japanese leaders with two alternatives: (1) they could give in to American demands that they withdraw from Manchuria or (2) they could thwart the embargo by attacking the U.S. fleet at Pearl Harbor and then seizing the oil supplies and other raw materials in Southeast Asia.

3. The Japanese attack on Pearl Harbor occurred after diplomatic negotiations with the United States had reached a stalemate.

> *Pearl Harbor is the only World War II battle that has appeared on an APUSH exam. Do not expect to see the Battle of the Bulge or the D-Day invasions appear as test questions.*

B. GERMANY FIRST

1. The Japanese attack unified America. Angry Americans vowed to avenge the treacherous attack on Pearl Harbor.

2. After the attack on Pearl Harbor, the United States announced a strategy of first defeating Germany and then turning to a full-scale attack on Japan. Although at first unpopular, the get-Germany-first strategy prevailed. The United States could not allow Hitler to defeat Great Britain and the Soviet Union, thus transforming the continent into an unconquerable Fortress Europe.

III. DIPLOMACY AND THE BIG THREE

A. LATIN AMERICA

1. Based upon the principles of the Good Neighbor Policy, the Roosevelt administration formally renounced the right to intervene in Latin America.
2. During World War II, the United States sought greater cooperation with the nations of Latin America, primarily to develop a hemispheric common front against fascism.

B. THE PHILIPPINE ISLANDS

1. In response to widespread anti-imperialist sentiments, the United States pledged to grant independence to the Philippine Islands.
2. The Philippines gained independence from the United States in 1946.

C. THE BIG THREE

1. The Big Three were Roosevelt, Churchill, and Stalin.
2. The Big Three demanded the unconditional surrender of Germany and Japan.
3. The Big Three held their final meeting at Yalta in February 1945.
4. The presence of Soviet troops in Poland limited President Roosevelt's options at the Yalta Conference.

IV. WARTIME MOBILIZATION OF THE ECONOMY

A. IMPACT OF MILITARY SPENDING

1. Military spending revived the U.S. economy.
2. As American industry prepared for war, unemployment plummeted.
3. The dramatic increase in military spending enabled the United States to finally emerge from the Great Depression.

B. PRICE CONTROLS

1. The government instituted direct price controls to halt inflation.
2. The Office of Price Administration (OPA) established a nationwide rationing system for consumer goods such as coffee and gasoline.

V. AFRICAN AMERICANS AND WOMEN

A. AFRICAN AMERICANS

1. The war years witnessed a continuing migration of African Americans from the rural South to urban centers in the North and West. Some 1.6 million African Americans left the South.
2. President Roosevelt issued an executive order forbidding discrimination in defense industries. The order was monitored by the Fair Employment Practices Commission.

B. WOMEN AND THE WORKPLACE

1. "Rosie the Riveter" was a nickname given during World War II to American women who did industrial work in the 1940s.
2. The war mobilization caused a significant movement of married women into the workforce.

Test Tip

Although you should not expect to find questions about battles and generals, you should prepare for questions about developments on the home front. There is a much greater chance that Rosie the Riveter will be on your exam than General Patton.

VI. CIVIL LIBERTIES AND CIVIL RIGHTS DURING WARTIME

A. THE INTERNMENT OF JAPANESE AMERICANS

1. In March 1942, President Roosevelt ordered that all Japanese Americans living on the West Coast be removed to "relocation centers" for the duration of the war.

2. Japanese Americans were sent to the internment camps on the grounds that they were, allegedly, a potential security threat.

B. *KOREMATSU v. UNITED STATES*

1. The relocation of Japanese Americans during World War II raised the constitutionality of the internment of Japanese Americans as a wartime necessity.
2. The Supreme Court ruling in *Korematsu v. United States* upheld the constitutionality of the internment of Japanese Americans as a wartime necessity.

VII. THE UNITED STATES AND THE ATOMIC BOMB

A. THE MANHATTAN PROJECT

1. President Roosevelt authorized the Manhattan Project.
2. President Truman authorized the use of the atomic bomb on the Japanese cities of Hiroshima and Nagasaki.
3. The United States was the only country possessing atomic bombs in 1945.

B. TRUMAN'S DECISION TO USE THE ATOMIC BOMB

1. Continuing to use conventional weapons would result in the loss of thousands of American lives.
2. Using the atomic bomb would persuade the Japanese to surrender.
3. Ending the war against Japan as quickly as possible would prevent Soviet intervention.
4. Using the atomic bomb would convince the Soviet Union of the need to be more cooperative in formulating its postwar plans.

THE

COLD WAR
—— 1945–1989

I. TRUMAN AND CONTAINMENT

A. KEY POINTS

1. Containment was a foreign policy designed to contain or block Soviet expansion.
2. Containment was the primary U.S. foreign policy from the announcement of the Truman Doctrine in 1947 to the fall of the Berlin Wall in 1989.

B. ROLE OF GEORGE KENNAN

1. George Kennan was an American diplomat and specialist on the Soviet Union.
2. Kennan wrote an influential article advocating that the United States focus its foreign policy on containing the spread of Soviet influence.

What comes to your mind when you think of containment? If you are like most APUSH students, you recall the Truman Doctrine, the Marshall Plan, and NATO. Don't overlook George Kennan. His widely circulated "long telegram" played a key role in persuading the Truman administration to adopt the policy of containment.

C. THE TRUMAN DOCTRINE

1. President Truman was determined to block the expansion of Soviet influence into Greece and Turkey.
2. On March 12, 1947, Truman asked Congress for $400 million in economic aid for Greece and Turkey.

3. Truman justified the aid by declaring that the United States would support "free peoples who are resisting attempted subjugations by armed minorities or by outside pressures." This sweeping pledge became known as the Truman Doctrine.

D. THE MARSHALL PLAN

1. World War II left Western Europe devastated and vulnerable to Soviet influence.
2. The Marshall Plan was a program of economic aid designed to promote the recovery of war-torn Europe while also preventing the spread of communist influence.
3. The Marshall Plan was an integral part of Truman's policy of containment. Here is an excerpt from Truman's speech justifying the Marshall Plan:

   "Our policy is directed not against any country or doctrine, but against hunger, poverty, desperation, and chaos. Its purpose should be the revival of a working economy in the world so as to permit the emergence of political and social conditions in which free institutions can exist. . . . Any government that is willing to assist in the task of recovery will find full cooperation, I am sure, on the part of the United States government."

E. THE NATO ALLIANCE

1. Ten Western European nations joined with the United States and Canada to form a defensive military alliance called the North Atlantic Treaty Organization (NATO).
2. The NATO alliance marked a decisive break from America's tradition of isolationism.

F. THE BERLIN AIRLIFT

1. Fearing a resurgent Germany, the Soviet Union cut off Western land access to West Berlin, located deep within the Soviet zone.
2. President Truman ordered a massive airlift of food, fuel, and other supplies to the beleaguered citizens of West Berlin.
3. The Berlin Airlift marked a crucial and successful test of containment.

II. THE COLD WAR IN ASIA: CHINA, KOREA, AND VIETNAM

A. THE "FALL" OF CHINA

1. Led by Mao Zedong, the Chinese Communists defeated the Chinese Nationalists and declared the People's Republic of China both an independent and a Communist nation.

2. The collapse of Nationalist China was viewed as a devastating defeat for America and its Cold War allies. The "fall" of China had the following consequences:

   ▶ *The United States refused to recognize the new government in Beijing.*

   ▶ *The United States interpreted the Chinese Revolution as part of a menacing Communist monolith.*

   ▶ *The "fall" of China contributed to the anti-Communist hysteria in the United States.*

B. THE KOREAN WAR

1. The United Nations and Korea

   ▶ *The Korean War began when North Korea invaded South Korea on June 25, 1950.*

   ▶ *President Truman took advantage of a temporary Soviet absence from the United Nations Security Council to obtain a unanimous condemnation of North Korea as an aggressor. The Korean War thus marked the first collective military action by the United Nations.*

   ▶ *It is important to note that the Korean War was fought under U.N. auspices. In contrast, the Vietnam War was not fought under U.N. auspices.*

2. A Limited War

   ▶ *The Korean War was a limited war that extended the containment policy to Asia.*

   ▶ *Stung by criticism that the Democratic Party had "lost" China, Truman was determined to defend South Korea.*

3. Truman's Firing of MacArthur

   ▶ *The Chinese entered the war when the U.N. forces approached the strategic Yalu River.*

▶ *General MacArthur disagreed with President Truman's policy of fighting a limited war. MacArthur publicly favored a blockade of the Chinese coast and bombardment of Chinese bases. Truman responded by relieving the insubordinate MacArthur of his command.*

4. Peace Agreement

▶ *The combatants finally signed an armistice in July 1953.*

▶ *The armistice set the border between North Korea and South Korea near the 38th parallel at approximately the prewar boundary.*

5. Truman's Integration of the Armed Forces

▶ *Prior to the Korean War, African Americans fought in segregated units.*

▶ *President Truman ordered the racial desegregation of the armed forces. The Korean War marked the first time American forces had fought in integrated units.*

Test Tip

President Truman's decision to desegregate the armed forces marked an important, but often overlooked, event. Be sure you make a mental note and remember this important milestone in the civil rights movement.

C. THE VIETNAM WAR, 1946–1963

1. Containment and Vietnam

▶ *Following World War II, the United States adopted a policy of containment to halt the expansion of Communist influence.*

▶ *American involvement in Vietnam grew out of the policy commitments and assumptions of containment.*

2. The French Withdrawal

▶ *Following World War II, the French continued to exercise influence and control over Indochina.*

▶ *Led by Ho Chi Minh, the Viet Minh defeated the French at the pivotal battle of Dienbienphu. Following their defeat, the French withdrew from Vietnam in 1954.*

▶ *The United States refused to sign the Geneva Accords and soon replaced France as the dominant Western power in Indochina.*

3. The Domino Effect

> ▸ *The United States believed that if one nation fell under Communist control, nearby nations would inevitably also fall under Communist influence.*

> ▸ *Here is how Secretary of State Dean Rusk explained the domino effect: "If Indo-China were to fall and if its fall led to the loss of all of Southeast Asia, then the United States might eventually be forced back to Hawaii, as it was before the Second World War."*

III. KEY COLD WAR EVENTS DURING THE EISENHOWER ADMINISTRATION

A. SPUTNIK

1. Launched by the Soviet Union in 1957, *Sputnik* was the first Earth-orbiting satellite.
2. *Sputnik* stunned America, prompting President Eisenhower to establish the National Aeronautics and Space Administration (NASA).
3. *Sputnik* made education an issue of national security. Congress responded by passing the National Defense Education Act. The legislation significantly expanded federal aid to education by funding programs in mathematics, foreign languages, and the sciences.

B. DIPLOMATIC CRISES

1. Egypt seized the Suez Canal.
2. Castro gained control over Cuba.
3. The Soviet Union shot down an American U-2 spy plane.

Test Tip

The Suez crisis, the rise of Castro, and the U-2 crisis were all very important events. However, this importance has yet to be reflected on APUSH exams. For now, it is enough to simply be able to identify the events.

IV. THE RISE AND FALL OF McCARTHYISM

A. BACKGROUND

1. Joseph McCarthy was a relatively unknown U.S. senator from Wisconsin who catapulted to national attention by making sensational accusations that the U.S. State Department was "thoroughly infested with Communists."
2. McCarthyism is the making of public accusations of disloyalty without sufficient evidence.

B. THE RISE OF McCARTHYISM

1. The following factors contributed to the rise of McCarthyism:
   - *Fears raised by the "fall" of China to Communism and the emergence of Mao Zedong as the leader of the People's Republic of China*
   - *Fears raised by the Soviet Union's development of an atomic bomb*
   - *Fears raised by President Truman's emphasis on a foreign policy designed to contain Soviet expansion*
   - *Fears raised by revelations that Soviet spies had infiltrated sensitive agencies and programs in the United States (Two spy cases seemed to add credibility to the fear.)*
2. The first case involved a former State Department official named Alger Hiss. It is interesting to note that a young California congressman named Richard Nixon played a key and highly publicized role in the investigation of Hiss.
3. The second case involved Ethel and Julius Rosenberg. The Rosenbergs were executed for secretly giving information to the Soviet Union about the U.S. atomic bomb project.

C. McCARTHY'S TACTICS

1. McCarthy directed his attack at alleged Communists and Communist sympathizers.
2. Senator McCarthy played on the fears of Americans that Communists had infiltrated the State Department and other federal agencies.

3. McCarthy's accusations helped create a climate of paranoia, as Americans became preoccupied with the perceived threat posed by the spread of Communism.

4. As a result of McCarthy's anti-Communist "witch hunt," millions of Americans were forced to take loyalty oaths and undergo loyalty investigations.

5. The fear of Communist infiltration even spread to the motion picture industry. Hollywood executives instituted a "blacklist" of about 500 entertainment professionals who were denied employment because of their real or imagined political beliefs or associations. The blacklist ruined the careers of many actors, writers, and directors.

6. Senator McCarthy cynically used the climate of fear for his own political advantage.

D. THE FALL OF JOSEPH McCARTHY

1. In 1954, Senator McCarthy accused the U.S. Army of being infiltrated by Communist sympathizers.

2. A huge national audience watched the Army-McCarthy Hearings. McCarthy's boorish conduct and lack of evidence turned public opinion against him. A few months later, the Senate formally condemned him for "conduct unbecoming a member."

3. McCarthy died three years later of chronic alcoholism.

Test Tip

The rise and fall of Senator Joseph McCarthy has generated a significant number of APUSH questions. Make sure that you review and study the key points listed above in the review of McCarthyism. Also, it is important to note that both Richard Nixon and John F. Kennedy began their political careers as outspoken opponents of Communism.

CHRONOLOGICAL REVIEW

THE
UNFINISHED FIFTIES

I. MILESTONES IN THE MODERN CIVIL RIGHTS MOVEMENT

A. PRESIDENT HARRY S. TRUMAN

1. President Truman issued an Executive Order desegregating the armed forces in 1948. This marked the most significant civil rights breakthrough of his administration.
2. The Dixiecrats walked out of the 1948 Democratic National Convention to demonstrate their opposition to President Truman's civil rights legislation.

B. *BROWN v. BOARD OF EDUCATION OF TOPEKA*, 1954

1. The Supreme Court ruled that segregation in public schools was a denial of the equal protection of the laws guaranteed in the Fourteenth Amendment.
2. The Supreme Court decision directly contradicted the legal principle of "separate but equal" established by *Plessy v. Ferguson* in 1896.
3. As a result of its victory in *Brown v. Board of Education of Topeka*, the NAACP (National Association for the Advancement of Colored People) continued to base its court suits on the "equal protection" clause of the Fourteenth Amendment.

C. PRESIDENT DWIGHT D. EISENHOWER

1. President Eisenhower sent federal troops to Little Rock's Central High School to enforce court-ordered desegregation.
2. Ike supported his decision by saying, "The very basis of our individual rights and freedoms rests upon the certainty that the President and the Executive Branch of Government will

support and insure the carrying out of the decisions of the Federal courts, even, when necessary, with all the means at the President's command."

3. Although President Eisenhower did send troops to Little Rock, he was not a vigorous supporter of civil rights legislation.

4. The primary power granted to the Civil Rights Commission in 1957 was the authority to investigate and report on cases involving discrimination.

D. DR. MARTIN LUTHER KING JR.

1. Dr. King's goal was a peaceful integration of the races in all areas of society.

2. Dr. King's theory of nonviolent civil disobedience was influenced by the writings of Henry David Thoreau.

3. Dr. King was head of the Southern Christian Leadership Conference (SCLC).

4. On December 1, 1955, Rosa Parks refused to give up her bus seat to a White passenger. Her refusal helped galvanize the Montgomery Bus Boycott led by Dr. King.

5. The following quote vividly expresses Dr. King's philosophy of nonviolence:

"The problem with hatred and violence is that they intensify the fears of the White majority, and leave them less ashamed of their prejudices toward Negroes. In the guilt and confusion confronting our society, violence only adds to chaos. It deepens the brutality of the oppressor and increases the bitterness of the oppressed. Violence is the antithesis of creativity and wholeness. It destroys community and makes brotherhood impossible."

Test Tip

APUSH test writers know that you can identify Dr. King, so they often use a challenging but tricky question, asking you to identify Dr. King as the leader of the Southern Christian Leadership Conference (SCLC). Do not confuse the SCLC with Stokely Carmichael's more confrontational Student Nonviolent Coordinating Committee (SNCC).

E. THE SIT-IN MOVEMENT

1. Students staged the first sit-ins in Greensboro, North Carolina, in 1960 to protest segregation in public facilities.
2. The sit-ins provide an excellent example of nonviolent civil disobedience.

II. PROSPERITY AND CHANGE

A. THE AFFLUENT SOCIETY

1. The decade after World War II was characterized by the following:
   ▸ *Unprecedented prosperity*
   ▸ *A population explosion known as the baby boom*
   ▸ *Rapid and extensive suburbanization*

B. WOMEN AND THE WORKPLACE

1. Following World War II, large numbers of women left their industrial jobs to make room for returning soldiers.
2. As Rosie the Riveter gave up her tools and returned home, the housewife became the new ideal for married women.
3. Television programs such as *I Love Lucy*, *Father Knows Best*, and *The Honeymooners* all portrayed women in their roles as housewives.

C. INTERSTATE HIGHWAYS AND THE GROWTH OF SUBURBIA

1. Passed during the Eisenhower administration, the Federal Highway Act of 1956 created the interstate highway system.
2. The Federal Highway Act of 1956 vastly accelerated the growth of suburbia.

III. SOCIAL CRITICS, NONCONFORMISTS, AND CULTURAL REBELS

A. SOCIAL CRITICS

1. Social commentators criticized the conformity of postwar culture. The leading social critics were:
   - ▸ *William H. Whyte*—The Organization Man
   - ▸ *David Riesman*—The Lonely Crowd
   - ▸ *Sloan Wilson*—The Man in the Gray Flannel Suit
   - ▸ *John Kenneth Galbraith*—The Affluent Society

2. Critics lambasted most television programs, calling the new medium a "vast wasteland."

B. NONCONFORMISTS

1. Led by Jack Kerouac, Beat Generation writers rejected middle-class culture and conformity.

2. In his book *On the Road*, Kerouac expressed the alienation and disillusionment he felt toward mainstream American culture.

> *Both the Lost Generation writers of the 1920s and the Beat Generation writers of the 1950s wrote about their alienation and disillusionment with American conformity and materialism.*

C. CULTURAL REBELS

1. Rock and Roll
   - ▸ *Rock and Roll first emerged during the 1950s.*
   - ▸ *Rock and Roll was inspired and strongly influenced by Black musical traditions, especially rhythm and blues.*

2. Abstract Expressionist Artists
   - ▸ *Abstract Expressionism emerged in New York City in the late 1940s and early 1950s.*
   - ▸ *Led by Jackson Pollock, Abstract Expressionist artists abandoned paintings that represented reality. Instead, they created works of art that expressed their state of mind.*

3. Movie Stars
   - ▸ *Movie stars such as James Dean and Marlon Brando symbolized youthful rebellion.*

THE
TUMULTUOUS SIXTIES

 I. **THE NEW FRONTIER AND THE GREAT SOCIETY**

A. THE NEW FRONTIER

1. The Election of 1960
   - *John F. Kennedy was a Roman Catholic—the first to be nominated since Al Smith's losing campaign in 1928.*
   - *The 1960 election was the first to include televised debates. Audiences estimated at 60 million or more watched each of the four debates between JFK and Richard Nixon.*

2. Camelot
   - *JFK was the youngest elected president in American history.*
   - *JFK challenged Americans to boldly enter the "New Frontier" of the 1960s.*
   - *Kennedy and his glamorous wife, Jacqueline, presided over an elegant White House that was soon nicknamed Camelot after the legendary court of King Arthur.*

B. THE GREAT SOCIETY

1. Primary Goals
   - *Use the federal government to enhance social welfare.*
   - *Use education and job training to help disadvantaged people overcome the cycle of poverty limiting their opportunities.*

2. Legislative Achievements
   - *The Civil Rights Act of 1964*
   - *The Voting Rights Act of 1965*
   - *Medicare and Medicaid*
   - *The War on Poverty*
   - *Programs offering significant federal aid to education*

3. Similarities Between the New Deal and the Great Society

▶ *Both the New Deal and the Great Society used the government to enhance social welfare.*

▶ *Both the New Deal and the Great Society included all of the following:*

Government-sponsored employment programs
Government support for the arts
Federal programs to encourage housing construction
Federal legislation to help the elderly

4. Differences Between the New Deal and the Great Society

▶ *Preschool education for disadvantaged children was an innovative Great Society program that was not an extension of a New Deal program.*

▶ *In contrast to the New Deal, the Great Society included federal legislation protecting the civil liberties of African Americans.*

Test Tip

It is very important to know the similarities and differences between the New Deal and the Great Society. Especially note that, unlike the New Deal, the Great Society included landmark laws that protected the civil liberties and voting rights of African Americans.

II. MOVEMENTS FOR CIVIL RIGHTS

A. THE CIVIL RIGHTS MOVEMENT

1. Leadership of Dr. Martin Luther King Jr.

▶ *In April 1963, Dr. King led a campaign against segregation in Birmingham, Alabama.*

▶ *Within a few days, Police Commissioner Eugene "Bull" Connor arrested Dr. King and other marchers. In his "Letter from Birmingham Jail," Dr. King argued that citizens have "a moral responsibility to disobey unjust laws." Dr. King believed that civil disobedience is justified in the face of unjust laws.*

▶ *Connor ordered his police to use attack dogs and high-pressure fire hoses to disperse civil rights marchers. Millions of horrified TV viewers watched what Dr. King called a "visual demonstration of sin."*

▸ *Outraged by the violence, President Kennedy called upon Congress to pass a comprehensive civil rights bill that would end legal discrimination on the basis of race.*

▸ *In August 1963, Dr. King led a massive March on Washington to support President Kennedy's bill. Appealing for racial harmony and social justice, Dr. King declared, "I have a dream that my four little children will one day live in a nation where they will not be judged by the color of their skin, but by the content of their character."*

▸ *On July 2, 1964, President Johnson signed the Civil Rights Act of 1964. This landmark legislation prohibited discrimination because of race, religion, national origin, or gender. The act banned racial discrimination in private facilities such as restaurants and theaters that are open to the public.*

2. The Sit-In Movement

▸ *Students staged the first sit-ins in Greensboro, North Carolina, in 1960 to protest segregation in public facilities.*

▸ *The sit-ins provide an excellent example of nonviolent civil disobedience.*

3. Black Power

▸ *The Black Power movement of the late 1960s advocated that African Americans establish control of their political and economic life.*

▸ *The most important Black Power leaders were Malcolm X, chief spokesman of the Nation of Islam; Stokely Carmichael, head of the Student Nonviolent Coordinating Committee (SNCC); and Huey Newton, head of the Black Panthers.*

B. THE WOMEN'S RIGHTS MOVEMENT

1. Betty Friedan

▸ *Betty Friedan was the author of* The Feminine Mystique *and the first president of the National Organization for Women (NOW).*

▸ *NOW was founded in 1966 in order to challenge sex discrimination in the workplace.*

▸ *Here is a famous excerpt from* The Feminine Mystique: *"The problem lay buried, unspoken, for many years in the*

*minds of American women. It was a strange stirring, a
sense of dissatisfaction, a yearning that women suffered
in the middle of the twentieth century in the United
States. Each suburban wife struggled with it alone. As she
made the beds, shopped for groceries, matched slipcover
material, ate peanut butter sandwiches with her children,
chauffeured Cub Scouts and Brownies, lay beside her
husband at night—she was afraid to ask even of herself
the silent question—'Is this all?'"*

▶ *It is important to note that this passage from* The
Feminine Mystique *reflects the fact that during the 1960s,
feminism tended to be a movement of middle-class women.*

*Be sure that you can identify Betty Friedan. A significant
number of APUSH questions are devoted to Friedan's role in the
women's rights movement.*

2. The Expansion of Women's Rights

All of the following contributed to the expansion of women's
rights since 1963:

▶ *The Equal Credit Opportunity Act of 1974*
▶ *The Supreme Court decision in* Roe v. Wade
▶ *Title VII of the Civil Rights Act of 1964*
▶ *Affirmative action regulations*

III. COLD WAR CONFRONTATIONS: LATIN AMERICA

A. LATIN AMERICA

1. The Alliance for Progress

▶ *The Alliance for Progress was initiated by President
Kennedy in 1961. It aimed to establish economic
cooperation between North America and South America.*
▶ *The Alliance for Progress was intended to counter the
emerging Communist threat from Cuba.*

2. The Bay of Pigs

▶ *President Kennedy inherited from the Eisenhower
administration a CIA-backed scheme to topple Fidel Castro
from power by invading Cuba with anti-Communist exiles.*

▸ *When the invasion failed, Kennedy refused to rescue the insurgents, forcing them to surrender.*

▸ *Widely denounced as a fiasco, the Bay of Pigs defeat damaged U.S. credibility.*

▸ *The Bay of Pigs failure, along with continuing American covert efforts to assassinate Castro, pushed the Cuban dictator into a closer alliance with the Soviet Union.*

▸ *Soviet Premier Khrushchev responded by secretly sending nuclear missiles to Cuba.*

3. The Cuban Missile Crisis

▸ *The Cuban Missile Crisis was precipitated by the discovery of Soviet missile sites in Cuba.*

▸ *The Soviets withdrew their missiles from Cuba in exchange for a promise from the United States not to attack Fidel Castro.*

▸ *As part of the negotiations to end the Cuban Missile Crisis, President Kennedy promised to refrain from a military invasion of Cuba.*

IV. COLD WAR CONFRONTATIONS: THE VIETNAM WAR

A. THE TONKIN GULF RESOLUTION, 1964

1. An Incident in the Gulf of Tonkin

▸ *The United States alleged that North Vietnamese torpedo boats launched an unprovoked attack against U.S. destroyers in the Gulf of Tonkin.*

▸ *The facts of what actually happened have never been fully explained.*

2. The Resolution

▸ *Congress responded to the unsubstantiated report of North Vietnamese aggression by passing the Tonkin Gulf Resolution overwhelmingly.*

▸ *The resolution authorized President Lyndon Johnson to "take all necessary measures to repel any armed attack against the forces of the United States and to prevent further aggression."*

▸ *The Tonkin Gulf Resolution gave President Johnson a "blank check" to escalate the war in Vietnam.*

▸ *Within a short time, President Johnson began to dramatically escalate the number of U.S. troops in Vietnam.*

B. THE TET OFFENSIVE, 1968

1. What Happened?

   ▸ *In late January 1968, the Viet Cong suddenly launched a series of attacks on 27 key South Vietnamese cities, including the capital, Saigon.*

   ▸ *The Viet Cong were eventually forced to retreat after suffering heavy losses.*

2. Consequences

   ▸ *The Tet Offensive undermined President Johnson's credibility.*

   ▸ *As a result of the Tet Offensive, public support for the war decreased and antiwar sentiment increased.*

V. THE ANTIWAR MOVEMENT AND THE COUNTERCULTURE

A. PROTESTING GROUPS

During the 1960s, the following groups protested various aspects of American society:

1. African Americans
2. American Indians
3. Women
4. Youth—The Woodstock music festival was a countercultural gathering.
5. Hispanic Americans

B. ISSUES

1. The Vietnam War
2. Exclusion of women from the mainstream of American life
3. Increasing bureaucratization and impersonality of American life
4. Marginal economic status of minorities
5. The materialism of American society

KEY POLITICAL EVENTS AND DEMOGRAPHIC TRENDS
— 1968 TO THE PRESENT

 I. **THE ELECTION OF 1968**

A. DISSENSION WITHIN THE DEMOCRATIC PARTY

1. The assassination of Robert Kennedy left the Democratic Party divided between supporters of Vice President Hubert Humphrey and Senator Eugene McCarthy.

2. Humphrey won the nomination, but antiwar demonstrations at the Democratic National Convention in Chicago forced Humphrey to lead a badly divided party into the fall election.

B. GEORGE WALLACE AND WHITE BACKLASH

1. George Wallace was the former governor of Alabama. He was a long-time champion of school segregation and states' rights.

2. Running as the candidate of the American Independent Party, Wallace's campaign appealed to Americans who were upset by the violence and civil disobedience associated with antiwar and civil rights demonstrations.

3. Wallace won five states in the South and received strong support in some Northern states.

C. THE RISE OF NIXON

1. The turmoil within the Democratic Party benefited former vice president Richard Nixon.

2. Nixon campaigned and won on a promise to restore law and order. He successfully appealed to many middle-class Americans fed up with years of riots and protest

APUSH test writers have written a number of questions on the pivotal 1968 presidential election. Interestingly, several of their questions have focused on the role of George Wallace. Be sure you know that Wallace was a segregationist who ran as a third-party candidate. His campaign showed that a number of voters were upset by antiwar demonstrators, Black Power militants, and government officials, whom Wallace derisively called "pointy-headed bureaucrats."

II. NIXON AND VIETNAM

A. THE DOVES DEMAND PEACE

1. Doves opposed the Vietnam War and staged massive demonstrations, demanding immediate troop withdrawals.
2. Senator William Fulbright was a leading Dove. He wrote a critique of the war entitled *The Arrogance of Power*.

B. HAWKS AND THE SILENT MAJORITY SUPPORT NIXON

1. Hawks supported the Vietnam War, believing that withdrawing troops would be tantamount to surrender.
2. The Silent Majority was the name given by President Nixon to the moderate, mainstream Americans who quietly supported his Vietnam War policies. Members of the Silent Majority believed that the United States was justified in supporting South Vietnam.

C. THE INVASION OF CAMBODIA, 1970

1. The Silent Majority favored gradual withdrawal from Vietnam.
2. Given that support, Nixon began to slowly withdraw American troops from Vietnam and replace them with newly trained South Vietnamese troops.
3. Withdrawal was known as Vietnamization; the policy promised to preserve U.S. goals and bring "peace with honor."
4. The United States invaded Cambodia. On April 29, 1970, President Nixon, suddenly and without consulting Congress, ordered American forces to join with the South Vietnamese army and clean out the Viet Cong sanctuaries in officially neutral Cambodia.

5. Nixon defended the action, saying that it was necessary to protect American forces and support Vietnamization.

D. KENT STATE, 1970

1. Stunned by the invasion, college students across the nation erupted in protest.
2. More than 1.5 million angry students shut down 1,200 campuses.
3. Disaster struck hardest at Kent State University in Ohio. A massive student protest led to the burning of the ROTC building. In response to the growing unrest, the local mayor called in the National Guard.
4. Nervous members of the National Guard fired into a crowd of protesters, killing four students and wounding nine.
5. The Kent State shootings triggered massive antiwar rallies across the United States.

E. ENDING THE VIETNAM WAR

1. Henry Kissinger, President Nixon's national security advisor and top negotiator in Vietnam, engaged in a series of secret negotiations with the North Vietnamese, aimed at reaching a negotiated settlement.
2. The United States and the North Vietnamese finally reached an armistice: The Paris Accords, January 1973.
3. The United States agreed to withdraw the last of its troops. In exchange, the North Vietnamese released over five hundred prisoners of war.

F. CONSEQUENCES OF THE VIETNAM WAR

1. The war affected the economy as follows:
   ▶ *The United States could not afford both President Johnson's Great Society programs and the Vietnam War.*
   ▶ *The combination of spending on the war and expensive social programs produced the high inflation rates of the late 1960s and 1970s.*

2. The war affected international involvements as follows:

▶ *The Vietnam War increased public skepticism toward international involvements.*

▶ *In 1973, Congress passed the War Powers Act, which stipulated that the president must inform Congress within 48 hours if U.S. forces are sent into a hostile area without a declaration of war.*

III. NIXON AND DÉTENTE

A. BACKGROUND OF DÉTENTE

1. The United States and the Communist world had been locked in a Cold War since the end of World War II.
2. The United States and the Soviet Union had experienced a series of tense Cold War confrontations that included the Berlin Airlift, the construction of the Berlin Wall, and the Cuban missile crisis.
3. Meanwhile, the United States had not formally recognized the Chinese Communist government.
4. Nixon and Henry Kissinger believed that the United States needed a new and more flexible foreign policy.
5. Détente called for a relaxation of tensions between the United States and the Communist world.

B. DÉTENTE AND CHINA

1. In late 1971, Nixon stunned the nation and the world by announcing that he intended to visit China, "to normalize relations between the two countries."
2. Nixon visited Beijing in February 1972. His trip to China marked a dramatic example of détente.

C. DÉTENTE AND THE SOVIET UNION

1. Just three months after becoming the first American president to visit China, Nixon became the first American president to visit Moscow.

2. Nixon's visit led to a series of agreements that reduced tensions between the United States and the Soviet Union. The most important agreements were:

  ▸ *The Strategic Arms Limitation Talks (SALT) (These talks led to the SALT I Treaty, which limited the number of intercontinental ballistic missiles and submarine-launched missiles each superpower could have in its arsenal.)*

  ▸ *A series of agreements that expanded trade between the two superpowers.*

IV. NIXON AND THE NEW FEDERALISM

A. BACKGROUND

1. The Great Society programs had led to a dramatic increase in federal influence and federal spending.
2. Nixon wanted to reduce the size and influence of the federal government.

B. THE NEW FEDERALISM

1. Known as the New Federalism, Nixon's plan called for distributing a portion of federal power to state and local governments.
2. Under a program called revenue sharing, state and local governments could spend their federal dollars however they saw fit, within certain limitations.

V. THE CARTER ADMINISTRATION

A. THE ECONOMY

1. Inflation was the primary domestic issue during the Carter administration.
2. During the 1970s, the American economy experienced both an increasing rate of inflation and a slowing of economic growth.
3. This combination of rising inflation and rising unemployment was called stagflation.

4. All of the following characterized the economy during the Carter administration:
   ‣ *Increasing unemployment*
   ‣ *Increasing inflation*
   ‣ *Increasing government spending*
   ‣ *Increasing prices of gasoline due to the 1973 Arab oil embargo and the 1979 revolution in Iran*
   ‣ *Increasing interest rates*

5. All of the following were causes of inflationary pressure during the 1970s:
   ‣ *Spending from the Vietnam War*
   ‣ *Rising energy costs*
   ‣ *Soaring federal budget deficits*
   ‣ *Rising healthcare costs*

B. FOREIGN POLICY

1. President Carter emphasized a foreign policy based on human rights.
2. Carter's human rights policy aroused global concern and helped make human rights an international issue.
3. Carter was responsible for the Camp David Accords.
   ‣ *In the summer of 1978, Carter invited the leaders of Egypt and Israel to Camp David—the presidential retreat in Maryland.*
   ‣ *After 12 days of intense negotiations, the leaders reached a peace agreement known as the Camp David Accords.*

C. THE 1980 ELECTION

1. The Iran hostage crisis played a key role in President Carter's defeat in the 1980 election.
2. Other factors that hurt Carter included the following:
   ‣ *Double-digit inflation*
   ‣ *The energy crisis*

VI. KEY POLITICAL EVENTS AND DEMOGRAPHIC TRENDS, 1980–PRESENT

A. THE RISE OF REAGAN

1. Like Jimmy Carter, Ronald Reagan capitalized on his status as a Washington outsider.
2. Key issues in the 1980 election included the following:
   ▶ *The Iranian hostage crisis*
   ▶ *The weak economy and high rate of inflation*
   ▶ *Hostility toward big government*
   ▶ *Call for a more conservative Supreme Court*

B. REAGANOMICS

1. President Reagan implemented a series of economic policies known as "Reaganomics" or supply-side economics.
2. Key goals were as follows:
   ▶ *Reduce federal tax rates for businesses and wealthy Americans (The Reagan tax cuts led to large increases in the incomes of wealthy Americans.)*
   ▶ *Reduce corporate tax rates and encourage private investment*
   ▶ *Promote economic growth by deregulating business*

C. DEMOGRAPHIC TRENDS

1. The 1970s witnessed a significant migration of Americans from the Frostbelt to the Sunbelt. This migration has continued to the present.
2. The South and West have experienced the greatest population gains since 1970.
3. The last 25 years have witnessed a significant increase in immigration from Latin America and Asia.
4. An aging population will ultimately threaten the long-term solvency of the Social Security system.

CHRONOLOGICAL REVIEW

D. CLINTON PRESIDENCY

1. The United States approved the North American Free Trade Agreement (NAFTA) creating a North American trade bloc.

2. The United States became a member of the World Trade Organization (WTO). The WTO provides a framework for negotiating and formalizing trade agreements. It replaced the General Agreement on Tariffs and Trade (GATT) formed in 1947.

E. THE ELECTION OF BARACK OBAMA, 2008

1. In November 2008, a record number of voters elected Barack Obama as the nation's 44th president.

2. Obama thus became America's first African American president.

APUSH tests typically include only a few questions covering the period from 1980 to the present. Questions on recent history have focused on Reaganomics, the key demographic trends listed above, and the key economic events from the Clinton administration also listed above. The 2008 election of Barack Obama marks a watershed event that will most likely turn up on future exams.

PART III:
KEY THEMES
and Facts

MILESTONES AND KEY FIGURES IN AFRICAN AMERICAN HISTORY
———— 1619–1865

I. **FROM SERVITUDE TO SLAVERY IN THE CHESAPEAKE REGION, 1619–1690**

A. INDENTURED SERVANTS

1. The "headright" system enabled Chesapeake tobacco farmers to obtain both land and labor by importing workers from England.

2. English indentured servants were the chief source of agricultural labor in Virginia and Maryland before 1675. They accounted for 75 percent of the 130,000 English immigrants to Virginia and Maryland during the seventeenth century.

B. BACON'S REBELLION, 1676

1. The rebellion exposed tensions between backcountry farmers and the tidewater gentry.

2. The rebellion prompted the tidewater gentry to reevaluate their commitment to the system of indentured servants.

Test Tip

Bacon's Rebellion has been featured in a number of multiple-choice and essay questions. Be sure you study the role Bacon's Rebellion played in the transition from indentured servants to slave labor.

C. THE BEGINNING OF SLAVERY

1. The profitable cultivation of tobacco required inexpensive labor.

2. Slave labor in colonial Virginia and Maryland spread rapidly in the last quarter of the seventeenth century, as Blacks displaced White indentured servants in the tobacco fields.

II. GROWTH OF PLANTATION ECONOMIES AND SLAVE SOCIETIES, 1690–1754

A. THE SLAVE TRADE

1. In the seventeenth and eighteenth centuries, the vast majority of Africans who survived the transatlantic passage ended up working on plantations in Brazil and the Caribbean.
2. The fewest slaves were brought into British North America.

B. SLAVERY IN THE AMERICAN COLONIES

1. Slavery was legally established in all 13 colonies by the early 1700s.
2. Although enslaved, Africans maintained cultural practices brought from Africa.
3. Tobacco was the most important cash crop grown in the Chesapeake colonies. Rice was the most important cash crop grown in South Carolina.
4. Factors responsible for the development of slavery in the Southern colonies included the following:
   ▸ *The supply of indentured servants from England became insufficient by the late seventeenth century.*
   ▸ *The spread of tobacco cultivation westward created a demand for labor.*
   ▸ *Few seventeenth- and early eighteenth-century White colonists viewed human bondage as morally unacceptable.*
   ▸ *As its maritime power increased, England wanted to compete in the profitable slave trade begun by the Portuguese and Dutch.*

C. THE STONO REBELLION, 1739

1. The Stono Rebellion was one of the earliest known acts of rebellion against slavery in America.

2. It was organized and led by slaves living south of Charleston, South Carolina. The slaves tried unsuccessfully to flee to Spanish Florida, where they hoped to gain their freedom.

> *The Stono Rebellion and Nat Turner's slave revolt (1831) were two of the most significant slave rebellions. Perhaps because it is much better known, Nat Turner's slave revolt has yet to attract attention from APUSH test writers. In contrast, the Stono Rebellion has been a frequent subject of questions.*

III. GROWTH OF SLAVERY AND FREE BLACK COMMUNITIES, 1776–1815

A. THE DECLARATION OF INDEPENDENCE

1. The Declaration of Independence did *not* call for the abolition of the slave trade.

B. THE NORTHWEST ORDINANCE OF 1787

1. The Northwest Ordinance of 1787 excluded slavery north of the Ohio River.
2. The Northwest Ordinance of 1787 was the first national document containing a prohibition of slavery.

C. THE CONSTITUTION

1. As written in 1787, the U.S. Constitution explicitly guaranteed the legality of slavery in every state.
2. The Three-Fifths Compromise was an agreement between the Southern and Northern states. Under the terms of this compromise, three-fifths of the population of slaves would be counted for enumeration purposes regarding both the distribution of taxes and the apportionment of the members of the U.S. House of Representatives.
3. The Fourteenth Amendment invalidated the Three-Fifths Compromise. The amendment specifically states, "Representatives shall be apportioned . . . counting the whole number of persons in each state."

D. THE HAITIAN SLAVE REBELLION

1. The Haitian slave rebellion of the 1790s prompted an increased fear of slave revolts in the South.

2. The rebellion was led by Toussaint L'Ouverture.

E. FREE AFRICAN AMERICANS

1. The following factors contributed to the growth of the free African American population:
   - *The gradual emancipation laws of individual states*
   - *Manumission granted for Revolutionary War service*
   - *Manumission granted by slaveholders' wills*
   - *Natural increase among free African Americans*

IV. PLANTERS AND SLAVES IN THE ANTEBELLUM SOUTH, 1816–1860

A. KING COTTON

1. The following factors contributed to making cotton the South's most important cash crop:
   - *The invention of the cotton gin made it possible and profitable to harvest short-staple cotton.*
   - *Rich new farmland in the Deep South was opened to the cultivation of cotton. By 1850, the geographic center of slavery was moving southward and westward.*
   - *The rise of textile manufacturing in England created enormous demand for cotton.*

B. SOUTHERN SOCIETY

1. It is very important to remember that a majority of White adult males were small farmers rather than wealthy planters.

2. The majority of White families in the antebellum South owned no slaves.

3. Nonetheless, a small minority of planters who owned 20 or more slaves dominated the antebellum South.

4. The cost of slave labor rose sharply between 1800 and 1860.

C. SLAVE SOCIETY

1. Despite forced separations, slaves maintained social networks among kindred and friends.

2. The dramatic increase in the South's slave labor force was due to the natural population increase of American-born slaves.

3. During the antebellum period, free African Americans were able to accumulate some property in spite of discrimination.

4. Although Southern legal codes did not uniformly provide for the legalization and stability of slave marriage, slaves were generally able to marry, and the institution of marriage was common on Southern plantations.

5. The majority of slaves adapted to the oppressive conditions imposed on them by developing a separate African American culture.

6. Slave revolts were infrequent. Most Southern slaves resisted their masters by feigning illness and working as slowly as possible.

V. TERRITORIAL EXPANSION AND SLAVERY, 1820–1860

A. THE MISSOURI COMPROMISE OF 1820

1. Provisions of the Missouri Compromise included the following:
   - *Maine would enter the Union as a free state.*
   - *Missouri would enter the Union as a slave state.*
   - *The remaining territory of the Louisiana Purchase above latitude 36° 30' would be closed to slavery.*

2. Consequences included the following:
   - *The number of Northerners and Southerners in the Senate remained the same.*
   - *Most of the Louisiana Purchase was closed to slavery.*
   - *The first major nineteenth-century conflict over slavery was settled.*
   - *Slavery was temporarily defused as a national political issue.*

B. TEXAS

1. President Jackson resisted the admission of Texas into the Union in 1836, primarily because he feared that the debate over the admission of Texas would ignite controversy over slavery.
2. Following a joint resolution of Congress, Texas joined the Union in December 1845.

C. THE WILMOT PROVISO

1. The Wilmot Proviso specifically provided for the prohibition of slavery in lands acquired from Mexico in the Mexican War.
2. Congress did *not* pass the Wilmot Proviso.

D. THE COMPROMISE OF 1850

1. California was admitted to the Union as a free state.
2. Slave trade (but not slavery) was abolished in the District of Columbia.
3. Territorial governments were created in New Mexico and Utah without an immediate decision as to whether they would be slave or free.
4. A stringent measure—the Fugitive Slave Act—was enacted. The act proved to be the most controversial and divisive component of the Compromise of 1850.

E. OSTEND MANIFESTO, 1854

1. The manifesto was a proposal to seize Cuba by force.
2. Enraged antislavery Northerners prevented it from being implemented.

F. THE KANSAS-NEBRASKA ACT, 1854

1. Provisions of the act included the following:
   - *The proposed Territory of Nebraska would be divided into two territories, Kansas and Nebraska.*
   - *The status of slavery would be settled by popular sovereignty.*
   - *Popular sovereignty meant that the settlers in a given territory would have the sole right to decide whether or not slavery would be permitted.*

▶ *Senator Stephen A. Douglas was the leading proponent of popular sovereignty. Here is how Douglas explained the doctrine of popular sovereignty: "The great principle is the right of every community to judge and decide for itself whether a thing is right or wrong. . . . It is no answer to this argument to say that slavery is an evil, and hence should not be tolerated. You must allow the people to decide for themselves whether it is a good or an evil."*

2. Consequences included the following:
   ▶ *The Kansas-Nebraska Act repealed the Missouri Compromise, thus heightening sectional tensions.*
   ▶ *The Kansas-Nebraska Act led to the demise of the Whigs.*
   ▶ *The Kansas-Nebraska Act led to the rise of the Republican Party and Abraham Lincoln.*
   ▶ *Kansas became the first test of popular sovereignty.*

G. THE DRED SCOTT DECISION, 1857

1. The Supreme Court ruled that Black people were not citizens of the United States and therefore could not petition the Court.
2. The Dred Scott decision established the principle that national legislation could not limit the spread of slavery into the territories.
3. By stating that Congress had no right to prohibit slavery in the territories, the Dred Scott decision repealed the Northwest Ordinance of 1787 and the Missouri Compromise of 1820.
4. The Dred Scott decision became a contentious issue during the Lincoln-Douglas debates.

H. THE POSITIONS OF THE REPUBLICANS AND DEMOCRATS ON SLAVERY

1. The Democratic Party was divided on the issue of expanding slavery into the territories.
2. The Republican Party opposed the extension of slavery into the territories. However, the Republicans acknowledged that slavery should be protected in the states where it already existed.

VI. ABOLITION AND THE ABOLITIONISTS, 1830–1860

A. THE SECOND GREAT AWAKENING

1. The religious spirit of the Second Great Awakening increased public awareness of the moral outrages perpetuated by slavery.
2. The Second Great Awakening contributed to the growth of the abolitionist movement.

B. AMERICAN COLONIZATION SOCIETY

1. The goal of the American Colonization Society was the return of freed slaves to Africa.
2. The leaders of the American Colonization Society were middle-class men and women.

C. WILLIAM LLOYD GARRISON

1. Garrison issued the first call for the "immediate and uncompensated emancipation of the slaves."
2. Here is a famous quote from the first issue of *The Liberator*: "Let Southern oppressors tremble . . . I will be as harsh as Truth and as uncompromising as Justice . . . I am in earnest— I will not retreat a single inch—and I WILL BE HEARD!"

D. FREDERICK DOUGLASS

1. Frederick Douglass was the most prominent Black abolitionist during the antebellum period.
2. Published in 1845, Douglass's autobiography, *Narrative of the Life of Frederick Douglass, an American Slave* exposed Americans to the horrors and inhumanity of slavery.
3. Although best known as an abolitionist, Douglass championed equal rights for women and Native Americans. He often declared, "I would unite with anybody to do right and with nobody to do wrong."

E. HARRIET BEECHER STOWE

1. Harriet Beecher Stowe wrote *Uncle Tom's Cabin*.
2. *Uncle Tom's Cabin* intensified Northern opposition to slavery. Only the Bible sold more copies.

VII. EMANCIPATION AND THE ROLE OF AFRICAN AMERICANS IN THE CIVIL WAR, 1861–1865

A. THE EMANCIPATION PROCLAMATION, 1863

1. President Lincoln refrained from taking action to emancipate slaves until the Civil War had been in progress for almost two years. Lincoln delayed because he wanted to retain the loyalty of the Border States.

2. The Union victory at Antietam gave Lincoln the opportunity to issue the Emancipation Proclamation.

3. The Emancipation Proclamation only freed slaves in the rebellious states.

4. The Emancipation Proclamation did *not* free slaves in the Border States.

5. The immediate effect of the Emancipation Proclamation was to strengthen the moral cause of the Union.

B. AFRICAN AMERICANS AT WAR

1. For most of the Civil War, African American soldiers were paid less than White soldiers of equal rank.

2. The South considered African Americans serving in the Union army as contraband.

MILESTONES AND KEY FIGURES IN AFRICAN AMERICAN HISTORY
1865–PRESENT

I. RECONSTRUCTION AND THE NEW SOUTH, 1865–1896

A. THE RECONSTRUCTION AMENDMENTS

1. The Thirteenth Amendment abolished slavery and involuntary servitude.
2. The Fourteenth Amendment had three key components:
    ▶ First, it made the former slaves citizens, thus invalidating the Dred Scott decision.
    ▶ Second, it stated, "nor shall any State deprive any person of life, liberty, or property without due process of law; nor deny to any person within its jurisdiction the equal protection of the laws."
    ▶ Third, it protected recently passed congressional legislation guaranteeing civil rights to former slaves.
3. The Fifteenth Amendment provided suffrage for Black males.

B. SHARECROPPERS

1. The majority of freedmen entered sharecropping arrangements with former masters and other nearby planters.
2. Sharecropping and the crop lien system led to a cycle of debt and depression for Southern tenant farmers.
3. The freedmen did *not* receive 40 acres each.

C. BLACK CODES

1. Black Codes were intended to place limits on the socioeconomic opportunities and freedoms open to Black people.
2. Black Codes forced Black Americans to work under conditions that closely resembled slavery.

D. THE COMPROMISE OF 1877

1. The compromise called for the removal of all federal troops from the South.
2. It supported internal improvements in the South.
3. It promised there would be at least one Southerner in the Cabinet.
4. It gave conservative Southern Democrats some control over local patronage.
5. It gave the South a "free hand" in race relations. As a result, White conservatives returned to power, lynchings increased, and Black voters were disenfranchised.

E. THE 1873 SLAUGHTERHOUSE CASES AND THE 1883 CIVIL RIGHTS CASES

1. Both cases narrowed the meaning and effectiveness of the Fourteenth Amendment.
2. Both cases weakened the protection given to African Americans under the Fourteenth Amendment.

F. *PLESSY v. FERGUSON*, 1896

1. The *Plessy v. Ferguson* decision upheld segregated railroad facilities.
2. The Supreme Court decision in *Plessy v. Ferguson* sanctioned "separate but equal" public facilities for African Americans.

G. DISENFRANCHISING BLACK VOTERS

1. Southern politicians used a number of tactics to disenfranchise Black voters; tactics included these:
    ▸ *Literacy tests and poll taxes were used to deny African Americans the ballot.*

> ▸ *The grandfather clause exempted from these requirements anyone whose forebear had voted in 1860. Needless to say, slaves had not voted at that time.*
> ▸ *Electoral districts were gerrymandered to favor the Democratic Party.*

H. BOOKER T. WASHINGTON

1. In his Atlanta Compromise speech (1895), Booker T. Washington called on Blacks to seek economic opportunities rather than political rights. Here is an excerpt from his speech: "In all things purely social we can be as separate as the fingers, yet one as the hand in all things essential to mutual progress."

2. Booker T. Washington particularly stressed the importance of vocational education and economic self-help. Washington urged Black Americans to avoid public political agitation.

3. Booker T. Washington supported all of the following:
   > ▸ *Accommodation to White society*
   > ▸ *Economic self-help*
   > ▸ *Industrial education*

4. Washington opposed public political agitation.

II. BLACK AMERICANS DURING THE PROGRESSIVE ERA, 1897–1917

A. W.E.B. DU BOIS

1. During the Progressive Era, W.E.B. Du Bois emerged as the most influential advocate of full political, economic, and social equality for Black Americans.

2. Du Bois founded the National Association for the Advancement of Colored People in 1909.

3. Du Bois advocated the intellectual development of a "talented tenth" of the Black population. Du Bois hoped that this talented tenth would become influential through methods such as continuing their education, writing books, or becoming directly involved in social change.

4. Du Bois opposed the implementation of Booker T. Washington's program for Black progress.

Be sure you understand the different approaches of Booker T. Washington and W.E.B. Du Bois. Remember, Washington stressed economic self-help, while Du Bois stressed fighting for full political and social rights.

B. THE NAACP

1. The National Association for the Advancement of Colored People (NAACP) rejected Booker T. Washington's gradualism and separatism.
2. The NAACP focused on using the courts to achieve equality and justice.

C. THE PROGRESSIVES

1. Civil rights laws for Black Americans were *not* part of the Progressive program of reforms.
2. Progressive Era legislation was *least* concerned with ending racial segregation.

D. IDA B. WELLS-BARNETT

1. Ida B. Wells-Barnett was an African American civil rights advocate and an early women's rights advocate.
2. Ida B. Wells-Barnett was the principal public opponent of lynching in the South.

E. THE BIRTH OF A NATION AND THE KKK

1. The Ku Klux Klan first emerged during Radical Reconstruction (1865–1877).
2. D. W. Griffith's epic film *The Birth of a Nation* (1915) became controversial because of its depiction of KKK activities as heroic and commendable.
3. *The Birth of a Nation* played a role in the resurgence of the KKK during the Progressive Era.
4. The KKK favored White supremacy and immigration restriction.

F. WORLD WAR I

1. African Americans fought in strictly segregated units, usually under the command of White officers.
2. The first massive migration of Black Americans from the South occurred during and immediately after World War I.

III. THE 1920s

A. THE HARLEM RENAISSANCE

1. The Harlem Renaissance thrived during the 1920s.
2. The Harlem Renaissance was an outpouring of Black artistic and literary creativity.
3. Harlem Renaissance writers and artists expressed pride in their African American culture.
4. Key figures in the Harlem Renaissance included James Weldon Johnson, Langston Hughes, Zora Neale Hurston, and Josephine Baker.

B. MARCUS GARVEY

1. Marcus Garvey was the leader of the Universal Negro Improvement Association.
2. Garveyism was identified with the following:
   - *Black pride*
   - *Black economic development*
   - *Black nationalism*
   - *Pan-Africanism*
3. Garvey was committed to the idea that Black Americans should return to Africa.

Frederick Douglass, Booker T. Washington, W.E.B. Du Bois, and Dr. Martin Luther King Jr. are America's best-known civil rights leaders. Each has been the subject of a number of APUSH questions. Although you should study these leaders, do not neglect Ida B. Wells-Barnett and Marcus Garvey. Recent tests have included questions about both of these important, but sometimes overlooked, leaders.

KEY THEMES AND FACTS

IV. THE GREAT DEPRESSION AND THE NEW DEAL, 1929–1941

A. THE NEW DEAL

1. New Deal programs did help African Americans survive the Great Depression.
2. The New Deal did *not* directly confront racial segregation and injustice. As a result, there was no major action on civil rights.

B. SHIFT IN VOTING PATTERNS

1. As a result of the Emancipation Proclamation and the Reconstruction amendments, African Americans were loyal voters for the Republican Party.
2. The presidency of Franklin D. Roosevelt witnessed a major shift of Black voters from the Republican Party to the Democratic Party.

C. ELEANOR ROOSEVELT AND THE DAR

1. In 1939, the Daughters of the American Revolution (DAR) barred Marian Anderson, a world-renowned African-American singer, from performing at Constitution Hall in Washington, D.C.
2. Outraged by this action, Eleanor Roosevelt resigned from the DAR.
3. Roosevelt's dramatic act of conscience gave national attention to the issue of racial discrimination.

V. WORLD WAR II, 1941–1945

A. HOMEFRONT

1. The Black migration from the South to the North and West continued.
2. President Roosevelt issued an executive order forbidding discrimination in defense industries. The order was monitored by the Fair Employment Practices Commission.

B. THE WAR

1. Black Americans continued to fight in segregated units. The armed forces were *not* racially integrated during World War II.

VI. THE MODERN CIVIL RIGHTS MOVEMENT, 1945–PRESENT

A. PRESIDENT HARRY S. TRUMAN

1. President Truman issued an Executive Order to desegregate the armed forces in 1948.
2. The Dixiecrats walked out of the 1948 Democratic National Convention to demonstrate their opposition to President Truman's civil rights legislation.

B. *BROWN v. BOARD OF EDUCATION OF TOPEKA*, 1954

1. The Supreme Court ruled that segregation in public schools was a denial of the equal protection of the laws guaranteed in the Fourteenth Amendment.
2. The Supreme Court decision directly contradicted the legal principle of "separate but equal" established by *Plessy v. Ferguson* in 1896.
3. As a result of its victory in *Brown v. Board of Education of Topeka,* the NAACP continued to base its court suits on the equal protection clause of the Fourteenth Amendment.

C. PRESIDENT EISENHOWER

1. President Dwight D. Eisenhower sent federal troops to Little Rock's Central High School to enforce court-ordered desegregation.
2. Ike supported his decision by saying, "The very basis of our individual rights and freedoms rests upon the certainty that the President and the Executive Branch of Government will support and insure the carrying out of the decisions of the federal courts, even, when necessary, with all the means at the President's command."

3. Although President Eisenhower did send troops to Little Rock, he was not a vigorous supporter of civil rights legislation.

4. The primary power granted to the Civil Rights Commission in 1957 was the authority to investigate and report on cases involving discrimination.

D. DR. MARTIN LUTHER KING JR.

1. Dr. King's goal was a peaceful integration of the races in all areas of society.

2. Dr. King's theory of nonviolent civil disobedience was influenced by the writings of Henry David Thoreau.

3. Dr. King was head of the Southern Christian Leadership Conference (SCLC).

4. In his "Letter from Birmingham Jail," Dr. King argued that citizens have "a moral responsibility to disobey unjust laws." Dr. King believed that civil disobedience is justified in the face of unjust laws.

5. The following quote vividly expresses Dr. King's nonviolent philosophy:

"The problem with hatred and violence is that they intensify the fears of the White majority, and leave them less ashamed of their prejudices toward Negroes. In the guilt and confusion confronting our society, violence only adds to chaos. It deepens the brutality of the oppressor and increases the bitterness of the oppressed. Violence is the antithesis of creativity and wholeness. It destroys community and makes brotherhood impossible."

E. THE SIT-IN MOVEMENT

1. College students staged the first sit-ins in Greensboro, North Carolina, in 1960 to protest segregation in public facilities.

2. The sit-ins provide an excellent example of nonviolent civil disobedience.

F. MALCOLM X

1. Malcolm X and Stokely Carmichael opposed Dr. King's strategy of nonviolent demonstration.

2. Malcolm X was a key leader of the Black Muslims.

G. KEY CIVIL RIGHTS LEADERS

1. Dr. King—Southern Christian Leadership Conference (SCLC)
2. Roy Wilkins—NAACP
3. Stokely Carmichael—Student Nonviolent Coordinating Committee (SNCC)
4. Black Panthers—Huey Newton
5. Black Muslims—Malcolm X

H. BLACK LEADERS WHO FAVORED SEPARATISM

1. Marcus Garvey—The Back-to-Africa Movement
2. Elijah Muhammad—The Black Muslim Movement
3. Stokely Carmichael—The Black Power Movement
4. Huey Newton—The Black Panther Movement

I. BLACK POWER

1. The Black Power movement of the late 1960s advocated that African Americans establish control of their economic and political life.
2. Huey Newton (Black Panthers) and Stokely Carmichael were spokesmen for Black Power.
3. The Black Panthers and the Nation of Islam emphasized a greater sense of Black nationalism and solidarity.

J. ELECTION OF BARACK OBAMA, 2008

1. In November 2008, a record number of voters elected Barack Obama as the nation's 44th president.
2. Obama thus became America's first African American president.
3. Obama's winning coalition included minorities, college-educated Whites, and young voters aged 18 to 26.

KEY THEMES AND FACTS

MILESTONES AND KEY FIGURES IN WOMEN'S HISTORY

I. **LIFE IN COLONIAL AMERICA, 1607–1789**

A. ANNE HUTCHINSON

1. Anne Hutchinson challenged Puritan religious authorities in Massachusetts Bay.
2. Puritan authorities banished Anne Hutchinson because she challenged religious doctrine, gender roles, and clerical authority, and she claimed to have had revelations from God.

B. LEGAL STATUS OF COLONIAL WOMEN

1. Women usually lost control of their property when they married.
2. Married women had no separate legal identity apart from their husband.
3. Women could *not* hold political office, serve as clergy, vote, or serve as jurors.
4. Single women and widows did have the legal right to own property.
5. Women serving as indentured servants had to remain unmarried until the period of their indenture was over.

C. THE CHESAPEAKE COLONIES

1. There was a scarcity of women and a high mortality rate among men. This was especially true in the seventeenth century.

2. As a result of the scarcity of women, the status of women in the Chesapeake colonies was higher than that of women in the New England colonies.

II. THE EARLY REPUBLIC, 1789–1815

A. ABIGAIL ADAMS

1. Abigail Adams was an early proponent of women's rights.

2. Here is an excerpt from the famous letter she wrote to her husband, John Adams:

   ". . . and by the way in the new code of laws which I suppose it will be necessary for you to make, I desire you would remember the ladies, and be more generous and favorable to them than your ancestors. . . . Remember, men would be tyrants if they could."

3. Abigail Adams's letter demonstrates that some colonial women hoped to benefit from republican ideals of equality and individual rights.

Test Tip

Sadly, John Adams ignored his wife's plea to "remember the ladies." Although ignored by the framers of the Constitution, Abigail's letter has been remembered by APUSH test writers. You should be able to identify the quote and know that some colonial women were committed to republican ideals.

B. THE CULT OF DOMESTICITY/REPUBLICAN MOTHERHOOD

1. The term *cult of domesticity* refers to the idealization of women in their roles as wives and mothers.

2. The term *republican mother* suggested that women would be responsible for rearing their children to be virtuous citizens of the new American republic. By emphasizing family and religious values, women could have a positive moral influence on the American political character.

3. Middle-class Americans viewed the home as a refuge from the world rather than a productive economic unit.

4. Catharine Beecher supported the cult of domesticity. Here is an illustrative quote:

"The mother writes the character of the future man; the sister bends the fibers that hereafter are the forest tree; the wife sways the heart, whose energies may turn for good or evil the destinies of a nation. Let the women of a country be virtuous and intelligent, and the men will certainly be the same."

III. WOMEN IN ANTEBELLUM AMERICA, 1815–1860

A. THE LOWELL SYSTEM

1. The Lowell System was a plan developed in the early nineteenth century to promote and expand textile manufacturing.
2. During the first half of the nineteenth century, textile mills in Lowell relied heavily on a labor force of women and children.
3. During the 1820s and 1830s, the majority of workers in the textile mills of Massachusetts were young unmarried women from rural New England who sought to earn money of their own.
4. Prior to the Civil War, Irish immigrants began to replace New England farm girls in the textile mills.

B. THE SENECA FALLS CONVENTION, 1848

1. The Seneca Falls Convention was organized and led by Elizabeth Cady Stanton and Lucretia Mott.
2. The Seneca Falls Convention called for women's rights in the following areas:
    ▸ *Suffrage*
    ▸ *The right to retain property after marriage*
    ▸ *Equal educational opportunities*
    ▸ *Divorce and child custody rights*
3. The "Declaration of Sentiments and Resolutions" issued by the Seneca Falls Convention demanded greater rights for women. The declaration's first sentence clearly states this goal: "We hold these truths to be self-evident: that all men and women are created equal."

C. CHARACTERISTICS OF THE WOMEN'S MOVEMENT IN THE ANTEBELLUM PERIOD

1. The movement was led by middle-class women.
2. It promoted a broad-based platform of legal and educational rights.
3. It had close links with the antislavery and temperance movements.
4. It held conventions in the Northeast and Midwest but not in the South.
5. It supported all of the following goals:
   ▸ *Right of women to vote*
   ▸ *Abolition of slavery*
   ▸ *Passage of temperance laws*
   ▸ *Right of married women to own property*

D. SARAH MOORE GRIMKÉ

1. She was one of the first women to publicly support abolition and women's suffrage.
2. Here is a famous quote by Grimké, advocating women's rights:

   "I ask no favors for my sex. I surrender not our claim to equality. All I ask of our brethren is that they will take their feet off our necks."

IV. REFORMERS AND SUFFRAGETTES, 1865–1920

A. JANE ADDAMS

1. Jane Addams is best known for founding Hull House in Chicago. (Note: Jane Addams was NOT an abolitionist.)
2. Hull House and other settlement houses became centers of women's activism and reform efforts to help the urban poor. Settlement house workers engaged in all of the following:
   ▸ *Teaching classes on cooking and dressmaking*
   ▸ *Publishing reports on deplorable housing conditions*
   ▸ *Offering literacy and language classes for immigrants*
   ▸ *Establishing day nurseries for working mothers*

B. THE FIGHT FOR SUFFRAGE

1. Frontier life tended to promote the acceptance of greater equality for women.

2. The only states with complete women's suffrage before 1900 were located west of the Mississippi. Wyoming (1869) was the first state to grant women the full right to vote.

3. The Nineteenth Amendment (1920) guaranteed women the right to vote.

C. THE WOMEN'S CHRISTIAN TEMPERANCE UNION (WCTU)

1. Carry Nation was one of the best known and most outspoken leaders of the WCTU.

2. The WCTU successfully convinced many women that they had a moral responsibility to improve society by working for prohibition.

D. WOMEN AND THE PROGRESSIVE REFORMS

1. Dorothea Dix worked tirelessly on behalf of the mentally ill.

2. Ida B. Wells-Barnett was an African American civil rights advocate and an early women's rights advocate. She is noted for her opposition to lynching.

3. Women reformers were also actively involved in the following Progressive Era reforms:
   ▸ *Passage of child labor legislation at the state level*
   ▸ *Campaigns to limit the working hours of women and children*

E. WOMEN AND THE WORKPLACE

1. During the late nineteenth and early twentieth centuries, the majority of female workers employed outside the home were young and unmarried.

2. During the late nineteenth and early twentieth centuries, women were most likely to work outside their homes as one of the following:
   ▸ *Domestic servants*
   ▸ *Garment workers*

> ▸ *Teachers*
> ▸ *Cigar makers*

3. During the late nineteenth century, women were least likely to work outside their homes as any of the following:
> ▸ *Physicians*
> ▸ *Lawyers*

V. BOOM AND BUST, 1920–1940

A. FLAPPERS

1. Flappers symbolized the new freedom by challenging traditional American attitudes about women. They favored short bobbed hair, smoked cigarettes, and even wore the new one-piece bathing suits.
2. In reality, few women actually lived the flapper lifestyle. Nonetheless, the look was very fashionable among college coeds, office workers, and store clerks.

B. WOMEN AND THE WORKFORCE

1. Although new jobs became available in offices and stores, the percentage of single women in the labor force actually declined between 1920 and 1930.
2. Women did not receive equal pay and continued to face discrimination in the professions.
3. Most married women did not seek employment outside the home.

C. MARGARET SANGER

1. Margaret Sanger was an outspoken reformer who openly championed birth control for women.

D. DECLINE OF THE FEMINIST MOVEMENT

1. The following factors caused a decline in the organized feminist movement during the 1920s:
> ▸ *The passage of the Nineteenth Amendment granting women the right to vote*

▸ *Changing manners and morality symbolized by the flappers*

▸ *Dissension among women's groups concerning goals*

▸ *The decline of the Progressive Era reform movement*

E. ELEANOR ROOSEVELT

1. Eleanor Roosevelt was a strong supporter of women's rights during the period of the New Deal.

The passage of the Nineteenth Amendment and the end of the Progressive Era left a great void in the struggle for women's rights. Margaret Sanger and Eleanor Roosevelt were the two best-known proponents of women's rights.

VI. WOMEN AND THE WORKPLACE, 1941–1960

A. WORLD WAR II

1. World War II stimulated a widespread movement of women into factory work.

2. During World War II, married women entered the workforce in large numbers.

3. "Rosie the Riveter" was a nickname given to women who worked in America's factories during World War II.

B. THE 1950s

1. Following World War II, women were encouraged to give up their factory jobs and return home, where they would devote themselves to being wives and mothers.

VII. THE MODERN WOMEN'S RIGHTS MOVEMENT

A. BETTY FRIEDAN

1. Betty Friedan wrote *The Feminine Mystique* and was the first president of the National Organization for Women (NOW).

KEY THEMES AND FACTS

2. Friedan was one of the founders of NOW—an organization founded in 1966 to challenge sex discrimination in the workplace.

3. Here is a famous excerpt from her book *The Feminine Mystique*:

"The problem lay buried, unspoken, for many years in the minds of American women. It was a strange stirring, a sense of dissatisfaction, a yearning that women suffered in the middle of the twentieth century in the United States. Each suburban wife struggled with it alone. As she made the beds, shopped for groceries, matched slipcover material, ate peanut butter sandwiches with her children, chauffeured Cub Scouts and Brownies, lay beside her husband at night—she was afraid to ask even of herself the silent question—'Is this all?'"

4. It is important to note that the passage from Friedan reflects the fact that feminism tended to be a movement of middle-class women.

5. Betty Friedan is best known for her criticism of traditional gender roles.

B. THE EXPANSION OF WOMEN'S RIGHTS SINCE 1963

1. All of the following contributed to the expansion of women's rights since 1963:
   ▸ *The Equal Credit Opportunity Act of 1974*
   ▸ *The Supreme Court decision in* Roe v. Wade
   ▸ *Title VII of the Civil Rights Act of 1964*
   ▸ *Affirmative action regulations*

C. THE EQUAL RIGHTS AMENDMENT (ERA)

1. The Equal Rights Amendment did not pass. So the ERA is *not* an amendment.

2. Phyllis Schlafly led a campaign to block ratification of the Equal Rights Amendment.

D. FEMALE VICE-PRESIDENTIAL CANDIDATES

1. Geraldine Ferraro was the first woman nominated for vice president by a major political party. She was Democrat Walter Mondale's running mate in 1984.

2. Sarah Palin was the first woman nominated for vice president by the Republican Party. She was John McCain's running mate in 2008.

MILESTONES IN NATIVE AMERICAN HISTORY

I. PRE-COLUMBIAN SOCIETIES

A. ARRIVAL IN NORTH AMERICA

1. Most scholars now believe that the first Native Americans reached North America by traveling across a land bridge connecting eastern Siberia and Alaska.

B. KEY ADVANCES

1. Pre-Columbian peoples developed all of the following:
   - *A mathematically based calendar*
   - *Irrigation systems*
   - *Domesticated cereal crops such as maize*
   - *Multifamily dwellings*
   - *Herbal medical treatments*
   - *Large cities such as the Aztec capital*

C. KEY FAILURES

1. Pre-Columbian peoples did *not* develop the following:
   - *Wheeled vehicles*
   - *Gunpowder*
   - *Waterwheels*

Test Tip

APUSH exams rarely if ever contain questions on Pre-Columbian peoples.

II. FIRST EUROPEAN CONTACTS WITH NATIVE AMERICANS

A. COLUMBIAN EXCHANGE

1. The term refers to the exchange of plants and animals between the New World and Europe following the discovery of America in 1492.

2. New World crops such as corn, tomatoes, and potatoes had a dramatic effect on the European diet. At the same time, Old World domesticated animals such as horses, cows, and pigs had a dramatic effect on life in the New World.

B. DISEASE AND POPULATION COLLAPSE

1. Old World diseases caused epidemics among the Native American inhabitants of the New World.

2. Native Americans suffered severe population declines because they lacked immunity to smallpox and other European diseases.

C. SIMILARITIES BETWEEN NATIVE AMERICANS AND THE FIRST ENGLISH SETTLERS

1. Both had agricultural economies.
2. Both lived in village communities.
3. Both domesticated corn and other vegetables.
4. Both shared a strong sense of spirituality.

D. DIFFERENCES BETWEEN NATIVE AMERICANS AND THE FIRST ENGLISH SETTLERS

1. Native Americans and English settlers had radically different conceptions of property.

2. The English had a very precise concept of private property rights.

3. Native Americans had no concept of private property.

E. INTERACTION BETWEEN NATIVE AMERICANS AND ENGLISH SETTLERS

1. The more Native Americans interacted with the English colonists, the more dependent they became on the fur trade.

2. Political and linguistic differences among Native Americans hindered united opposition to the English.

F. THE IROQUOIS CONFEDERACY

1. The Iroquois Confederacy was the most important and powerful Native American alliance.
2. The tribes of the Iroquois Confederacy formed the most important Native American political organization to confront the colonists.
3. During the eighteenth century, the Iroquois lived in permanent settlements.

Test Tip

As a general rule, APUSH test writers do not expect you to know the names of specific Native American tribes. The Iroquois are the one exception to this rule. Be sure that you can identify the Iroquois Confederacy.

III. FORCED REMOVAL OF AMERICAN INDIANS TO THE TRANS-MISSISSIPPI WEST

A. *WORCESTER v. GEORGIA* (1831)

1. The Cherokee differed from other Native American tribes in that the Cherokee tried to mount a court challenge to a removal order.
2. In the case of *Worcester v. Georgia,* the U.S. Supreme Court upheld the rights of the Cherokee tribe to their tribal lands.

B. ANDREW JACKSON AND THE CHEROKEES

1. President Jackson refused to recognize the Court's decision; he said, "John Marshall has made his decision: now let him enforce it."
2. Jackson's antipathy toward Native Americans was well known: "I have long viewed treaties with American Indians as an absurdity not to be reconciled to the principles of our government."

KEY THEMES AND FACTS

C. THE TRAIL OF TEARS

1. Jackson's Native American policy resulted in the removal of the Cherokee from their homeland to settlements across the Mississippi River.
2. The Trail of Tears refers to the relocation of Native Americans to settlements in what is now Oklahoma.
3. Approximately one-quarter of the Cherokee people died on the Trail of Tears.

IV. GOVERNMENT POLICY TOWARD AMERICAN INDIANS IN THE SECOND HALF OF THE NINETEENTH CENTURY

A. DECLINE OF THE PLAINS INDIANS

1. All of the following factors contributed to the decline of the Plains Indians:
    ▸ *The slaughter of 70 million buffalo*
    ▸ *The spread of epidemic diseases*
    ▸ *Construction of the railroads*

B. PUBLICATION OF *CENTURY OF DISHONOR* (1881)

1. The book was written by Helen Hunt Jackson.
2. It aroused public awareness of the wrongs that the federal government had inflicted on Native Americans.

C. DAWES ACT OF 1887

1. The Dawes Act was a misguided attempt to reform the government's Native American policy.
2. The legislation's goal was to assimilate Native Americans into the mainstream of American life. It attempted to accomplish this goal by doing the following:
    ▸ *Dissolving many tribes as legal entities*
    ▸ *Eliminating tribal ownership of land*
    ▸ *Granting 160 acres to individual family heads*

D. CONSEQUENCES OF THE DAWES ACT

1. The Dawes Act ignored the inherent reliance of traditional Indian culture on tribally held land.

2. By 1900, Indians had lost 50 percent of the 156 million acres they had held just two decades earlier.

3. The forced-assimilation doctrine of the Dawes Act remained the cornerstone of the government's official Indian policy for nearly half a century.

4. The Indian Reorganization Act of 1934 (often called the Indian New Deal) partially reversed the individualistic approach of the Dawes Act by restoring the tribal basis of Indian life.

Test Tip

APUSH test writers will not test you on the legendary battles between the Plains Indians and the U.S. Cavalry. However, they will expect you to be able to identify Helen Hunt Jackson's book **Century of Dishonor** *and be able to discuss the Dawes Act.*

E. THE GHOST DANCE

1. The dance was a sacred ritual expressing a vision that the buffalo would return and all the elements of White civilization would disappear.

2. Fearing that the ceremony would trigger an uprising, the army attempted to stamp it out at the so-called Battle of Wounded Knee.

3. As many as two hundred Indian men, women, and children were killed in the Battle of Wounded Knee.

V. CONTRIBUTIONS DURING WORLD WAR II

A. THE HOMEFRONT

1. Native Americans volunteered to work in defense industries.

B. THE NAVAJO CODE TALKERS

1. Fewer than 30 non-Navajos understood the Navajo's unwritten language.

2. Approximately 400 Navajos served as Code Talkers in the Pacific Theater. Their primary job was to transmit vital battlefield information via telegraphs and radios in their native dialect.

3. The Navajo Code Talkers saved countless lives and played a key role in the battle of Iwo Jima.

KEY SUPREME COURT CASES AND FAMOUS TRIALS

1. The Marshall Court, 1801–1835
   - *John Marshall believed that the United States would be best served by concentrating power in a strong central government.*
   - *Under Chief Justice John Marshall, Supreme Court decisions tended to promote business enterprise.*
   - *Under John Marshall's leadership, the Supreme Court upheld the supremacy of federal legislation over state legislation.*

2. *Marbury v. Madison, 1803*
   - *The case established the principle of judicial review.*
   - *Judicial review gave the Supreme Court the authority to declare acts of Congress unconstitutional.*
   - Marbury v. Madison *was one of a series of landmark decisions by Chief Justice John Marshall that strengthened the federal government.*

3. *Dartmouth College v. Woodward, 1819*
   - *The Supreme Court ruled that the Constitution protected contracts from state encroachments.*
   - *The ruling safeguarded business enterprise from interference by state governments.*

4. *Worcester v. Georgia, 1831*
   - *The Supreme Court upheld the rights of the Cherokee tribe.*
   - *President Jackson refused to recognize the Court's decision. He said "John Marshall has made his decision: now let him enforce it."*
   - *Because of Jackson's refusal to enforce the Supreme Court decision, the case was followed by the removal of the Cherokees from Georgia.*

Test Tip

APUSH test writers expect you to be able to identify the Marshall Court and its key decisions. Remember, John Marshall was a judicial nationalist who opposed states' rights.

5. *Dred Scott v. Sanford, 1857*
   ▶ *African Americans were not citizens and therefore could not petition the Court.*
   ▶ *Slaves could not be taken from their masters, regardless of a territory's "free" or "slave" status.*
   ▶ *The case was a major issue during the Lincoln-Douglas debates.*
   ▶ *The judge ruled that national legislation could not limit the spread of slavery in the territories.*
   ▶ *The Dred Scott decision invalidated the Northwest Ordinance and the 36° 30' line in the Missouri Compromise.*
   ▶ *Here is a quote from the* Dred Scott v. Sanford *case:*
   ". . . the descendants of Africans who were imported into this country, and sold as slaves . . . are not included, and were not intended to be included, under the word 'citizens' in the Constitution, and can therefore claim none of the rights and privileges which that instrument provides for and secures to citizens of the United States."
   ▶ *The Fourteenth Amendment invalidated the Dred Scott decision.*

6. The 1873 Slaughterhouse Cases and the 1883 Civil Rights Cases
   ▶ *Both cases narrowed the meaning and effectiveness of the Fourteenth Amendment.*
   ▶ *Both cases weakened the protection given to African Americans under the Fourteenth Amendment.*

7. *Plessy v. Ferguson, 1896*
   ▶ *The case involved a dispute over the legality of segregated railroad cars in Louisiana.*
   ▶ *It upheld segregation by approving "separate but equal" accommodations for African Americans.*
   ▶ *It sanctioned "separate but equal" public facilities for African Americans.*

8. Late Nineteenth- and Early Twentieth-Century Cases
   ▶ *Supreme Court decisions strengthened the position of big business.*

9. Sacco and Vanzetti Trial, 1920s
    ▸ *The trial illustrated the widespread fear of radicals and recent immigrants.*

10. The John T. Scopes Trial, 1925
    ▸ *The immediate issue was the legality of a Tennessee law prohibiting the teaching of the theory of evolution in the state's public schools.*
    ▸ *John T. Scopes was a Tennessee high school biology teacher, indicted for teaching evolution.*
    ▸ *The John T. Scopes trial illustrates the cultural conflict in the 1920s between fundamentalism and modernism.*

11. *Korematsu v. United States*, 1944
    ▸ *In early 1942, Japanese Americans living on the West Coast of the United States were forced from their homes into detention camps on the grounds that they were a potential threat to the security of the United States.*
    ▸ *The Supreme Court upheld the constitutionality of the relocation as a wartime necessity. Constitutional scholars now view the relocation as a flagrant violation of civil liberties.*

12. The Warren Court, 1953–1969
    ▸ *During a period of intense judicial activism, the Court used its power to promote social programs.*
    ▸ *The Warren Court reached notable and controversial decisions that established rights for those accused of crimes.*

13. *Brown v. Board of Education of Topeka*, 1954
    ▸ *The ruling reversed the principle of "separate but equal" established in* Plessy v. Ferguson.
    ▸ *It declared racially segregated public schools inherently unequal.*
    ▸ *It declared that public school segregation is a denial of equal protection of the laws under the Fourteenth Amendment.*
    ▸ *Remember, the Fourteenth Amendment guarantees citizens "equal protection of the laws." The Fourteenth Amendment is a key tool used by civil rights groups to overturn segregation.*
    ▸ *This was the most important Supreme Court decision in the decade following World War II. It had widespread consequences for the rights of minority groups.*

Test Tip

The Dred Scott Case, Plessy v. Ferguson, *and* Brown v. Board of Education of Topeka *form a triumvirate of key civil rights cases. You can expect to see one or two of these cases on every APUSH exam. Be sure to study the key points about each case.*

14. *Baker v. Carr, 1962*
    ▸ *The case established the principle of "one man, one vote."*
    ▸ *The Supreme Court required the reapportionment of districts for some state legislatures.*

15. *Griswold v. Connecticut, 1965*
    ▸ *The Supreme Court struck down a state law prohibiting the use of contraceptives.*
    ▸ *The Court proclaimed a "right to privacy" that soon provided the basis for decisions protecting women's abortion rights.*

16. *Miranda v. Arizona, 1966*
    ▸ *Controversial Warren Court decision establishing a defendant's "Miranda Rights."*
    ▸ *The Court ruled that no confession could be admissible unless a suspect had been made aware of his or her rights and the suspect had then waived them.*

17. *Roe v. Wade, 1973*
    ▸ *The U.S. Supreme Court upheld abortion rights for women.*
    ▸ *The Court based its decision, in part, on the right to privacy established in* Griswold v. Connecticut.

KEY WORKS OF LITERATURE, ART, AND MUSIC

1. *The Last of the Mohicans, 1757*
   ▶ *The novel was written by James Fenimore Cooper.*
   ▶ *It was part of a series of novels known as the* Leatherstocking Tales.
   ▶ *Cooper was the first American writer to feature uniquely American characters.*
   ▶ *Cooper created the first genuine Western heroes in American literature.*
   ▶ *Cooper's novels gave expression to the concept of the "noble savage."*

> Don't memorize works of literature and their authors. APUSH test writers rarely ask you to match a novel with its author. The authors are included here for easy reference. Instead, focus your studies on why the work of literature is important and what it illustrates about the time it was written.

2. "Common Sense," 1776
   ▶ *This was a pamphlet written by Thomas Paine.*
   ▶ *It was a strongly worded call for independence from Great Britain.*
   ▶ *Paine opposed monarchy (he called King George a Pharaoh!) and strongly favored republican government.*
   ▶ *Paine offered a vigorous defense of republican principles.*
   ▶ *Paine helped overcome the loyalty many still felt for the monarchy and mother country.*
   ▶ *Paine used biblical analogies and references to illustrate his arguments.*

3. The Federalist Papers (*The Federalist*), 1787
   ▶ *The Federalist Papers were written by Hamilton, Madison, and Jay to support ratification of the Constitution of 1787.*

KEY THEMES AND FACTS

▸ *They challenged the conventional political wisdom of the eighteenth century when they asserted that a large republic offered the best protection of minority rights.*

4. *The Liberator, 1831*
   ▸ *This newspaper was written and published by William Lloyd Garrison.*
   ▸ *It called for the "immediate and uncompensated emancipation of the slaves."*
   ▸ *Here is a famous quote from* **The Liberator:**
   "Let Southern oppressors tremble . . . I will be as harsh as Truth and as uncompromising as Justice . . . I am in earnest – I will not retreat a single inch—and I WILL BE HEARD!"

5. *Democracy in America, 1835*
   ▸ *Alexis de Tocqueville was the author.*
   ▸ *He argued that American individualism arose as a result of the absence of an aristocracy.*

6. The Hudson River School (mid-1800s)
   ▸ *The Hudson River School was a group of artists led by Thomas Cole, who painted landscapes emphasizing America's natural beauty.*
   ▸ *The Hudson River School was America's first coherent school of art.*

7. McGuffey Readers, 1836
   ▸ *William Holmes McGuffey was the compiler and editor*
   ▸ *Also known as Eclectic Reader*
   ▸ *The best known and most widely used reading instruction books in the nineteenth century. It is estimated that during this time four-fifths of all American school children used McGuffey readers.*
   ▸ *The McGuffey Readers featured stories, poems, and essays supporting patriotism and moral values.*

8. "Civil Disobedience: On the Duty of Civil Disobedience," 1849
   ▸ *Henry David Thoreau was the author of this essay.*
   ▸ *He expressed opposition to the Mexican War.*
   ▸ *Thoreau argued that individuals have a moral responsibility to oppose unjust laws and unjust actions by governments.*
   ▸ *Thoreau's essay influenced Dr. King's philosophy of nonviolent civil disobedience.*

9. *The Scarlet Letter, 1850*
   ▸ *Nathaniel Hawthorne was the author.*
   ▸ *The novel dealt with the legacy of Puritanism.*

10. *Leaves of Grass*, 1855
    ▶ *Walt Whitman was the author.*
    ▶ *Whitman's poems featured the Romantic movement's revolt against reason and embrace of nature*

11. *Uncle Tom's Cabin*, 1852
    ▶ *Harriet Beecher Stowe was the author.*
    ▶ *The novel strengthened Northern opposition to slavery.*
    ▶ *It was second only to the Bible in sales.*

12. *Walden*, 1854
    ▶ *Henry David Thoreau was the author.*
    ▶ *The novel espoused transcendentalism—that is, truth through inner reflection and exposure to nature.*
    ▶ *It recorded Thoreau's thoughts concerning the value of a life of simplicity and contemplation.*

13. Horatio Alger Jr. Stories (1867–1899)
    ▶ *Horatio Alger Jr. was the author.*
    ▶ *This is a collection of approximately 270 dime novels.*
    ▶ *Alger's novels feature rags-to-riches stories describing how down-and-out boys become rich and successful through hard work, honesty, and a little luck.*

14. *A Century of Dishonor*, 1881
    ▶ *Helen Hunt Jackson was the author.*
    ▶ *The book aroused public awareness of the federal government's long record of betraying and cheating Native Americans.*

15. *The Influence of Sea Power upon History*, 1890
    ▶ *Captain Alfred Mahan was the author.*
    ▶ *He argued that control of the sea was the key to world dominance.*
    ▶ *The book was very influential in promoting the growth of U.S. naval power during the late nineteenth century.*

16. *How the Other Half Lives*, 1890
    ▶ *Jacob Riis was the author.*
    ▶ *Riis was a journalist and photographer working primarily in New York City.*
    ▶ *Riis's book* How the Other Half Lives *provided poignant pictures that gave a human face to the poverty and despair experienced by immigrants living in New York City's Lower East Side.*

17. "The Significance of the Frontier in American History," 1893
    ▸ *Frederick Jackson Turner wrote this paper.*
    ▸ *He argued that the development of American individualism and democracy was shaped by the frontier experience.*
    ▸ *Turner's "frontier thesis" focused on the importance of the absence of a feudal aristocracy. In other words, America did not have a hereditary landed nobility.*
    ▸ *Here is a famous excerpt:*
    "From the beginning of the settlement of America, the frontier regions have exercised a steady influence toward democracy. . . . American democracy is fundamentally the outcome of the experience of the American people in dealing with the West. . . ."

18. *The Wonderful Wizard of Oz, 1900*
    ▸ *L. Frank Baum was the author.*
    ▸ The Wonderful Wizard of Oz *was originally written as a political commentary on free silver and the plight of American farmers.*

19. The Ashcan School of Art, early 1900s
    ▸ *This was a group of eight American artists, led by John Sloan.*
    ▸ *Ashcan artists focused on depicting urban scenes such as crowded tenements and boisterous barrooms.*

20. *The Jungle, 1906*
    ▸ *Upton Sinclair was the author.*
    ▸ *The novel exposed appalling conditions in the Chicago meatpacking industry.*
    ▸ *It was a classic example of a muckraking novel.*
    ▸ *The novel helped bring about passage of the Pure Food and Drug Act and the Meat Inspection Act of 1906.*

21. *Pragmatism, 1907*
    ▸ *William James was the author.*
    ▸ *His concept of pragmatism held that truth was to be tested, above all, by the practical consequences of an idea, by action rather than theories.*
    ▸ *In short, beliefs should be tested by experience. The ultimate test of truth is experience, not logic.*
    ▸ *It is important to remember that William James and other pragmatists do* not *believe in the existence of absolute truth.*

22. Lost Generation of the 1920s
    - ▶ *Key writers included Sinclair Lewis and F. Scott Fitzgerald.*
    - ▶ *This was called the Lost Generation because they were disillusioned with American society during the 1920s.*
    - ▶ *They criticized middle-class conformity and materialism. For example, Sinclair Lewis criticized middle-class life in novels such as* Babbitt *and* Main Street.

23. Harlem Renaissance, 1920s
    - ▶ *Key writers included Langston Hughes, Zora Neale Hurston, Claude McKay, Josephine Baker, and James Weldon Johnson.*
    - ▶ *They created distinctive African American literature.*
    - ▶ *Writers expressed pride in their African American culture.*

24. Jazz
    - ▶ *Black musicians such as Joseph ("Joe") King Oliver, W. C. Handy, and "Jelly Roll" Morton helped create jazz.*
    - ▶ *Jazz was especially popular among the youth because it symbolized a desire to break with tradition.*

25. *The Grapes of Wrath*, 1939
    - ▶ *John Steinbeck was the author.*
    - ▶ *Describes the plight of "Okies" forced to leave Dust Bowl-stricken Oklahoma in a futile attempt to find work in California.*

26. *The Organization Man*, 1956
    - ▶ *W. H. Whyte was the author.*
    - ▶ *The novel criticizes the homogenous culture of the 1950s.*
    - ▶ *It criticizes American conformity and the belief that economic growth would solve all problems.*

27. *On the Road*, 1957
    - ▶ *Jack Kerouac was the author.*
    - ▶ *The novel expressed the alienation and disillusionment of the Beat Generation of the 1950s.*
    - ▶ *Like other Beat Generation writers, Kerouac rejected middle-class conformity and materialism.*

28. Rock and Roll, 1950s
    - ▶ *Key musicians included Little Richard, Chuck Berry, and Elvis Presley.*
    - ▶ *Rock and roll first emerged during the 1950s.*

▶ Rock and roll was inspired and strongly influenced by Black musical traditions, especially rhythm and blues.

29. *Silent Spring* (1962)

▶ Rachel Carson was the author.

▶ Her work protested the contamination of the air, land, and water with chemical insecticides such as DDT.

▶ The novel played a key role in sparking the environmental movement in the United States.

Test Tip

Pay special attention to Rachel Carson and her watershed work **Silent Spring**. *APUSH test writers believe you should know this work. Rachel Carson was a woman of courage and conviction who alerted the public to the threat of chemical insecticides.* **Silent Spring** *aroused concerned Americans and helped launch the environmental movement.*

30. *The Other America*, 1962

▶ Michael Harrington was the author.

▶ Poignant and influential report on poverty in America

▶ The book played an important role in awakening JFK's interest in the poor and showed the way for LBJ's War on Poverty.

31. "Letter from Birmingham Jail," 1963

▶ The letter was by Dr. Martin Luther King Jr.

▶ Dr. King argued that citizens have *"a moral responsibility to disobey unjust laws."* Civil disobedience is thus a justified response to unjust laws.

KEY FACTS ABOUT LABOR UNIONS, LABOR LAWS, AND LABOR STRIKES

1. THE KNIGHTS OF LABOR
   ▶ *Under Terence V. Powderly's leadership, the Knights grew rapidly, peaking at 730,000 members in 1886.*
   ▶ *The Knights grew rapidly because of a combination of their open-membership policy, the continuing industrialization of the American economy, and the growth of urban population.*
   ▶ *The Knights welcomed unskilled and semiskilled workers, including women, immigrants, and African Americans.*
   ▶ *The Knights were idealists who believed they could eliminate conflict between labor and management. Their goal was to create a cooperative society in which laborers, not capitalists, owned the industries in which they worked.*
   ▶ *The Haymarket Square riot was unfairly blamed on the Knights. As a result, the public associated them with anarchists.*

2. THE INDUSTRIAL WORKERS OF THE WORLD (IWW)
   ▶ *The IWW was led by "Mother" Jones, Elizabeth Flynn, Big Bill Haywood, and Eugene Debs.*
   ▶ *Like the Knights of Labor, the IWW strove to unite all laborers, including unskilled workers and African Americans, who were excluded from craft unions.*
   ▶ *The IWW's motto was "An injury to one is an injury to all," and its goal was to create "One Big Union."*
   ▶ *Unlike the Knights, the IWW (or Wobblies) embraced the rhetoric of class conflict and endorsed violent tactics.*
   ▶ *IWW membership probably never exceeded 150,000 workers. The organization collapsed during World War I.*

Test Tip

Eugene Debs was one of the founders of the IWW. He was also one of the best-known socialist leaders in America. In a socialist system, the government owns the nation's basic industries and natural resources.

3. **THE AMERICAN FEDERATION OF LABOR (AFL)**

   ▸ *The AFL was led by Samuel Gompers, the leader of the Cigar Makers Union.*

   ▸ *The AFL was an alliance of skilled workers in craft unions.*

   ▸ *Under Gompers's leadership, the AFL concentrated on bread-and-butter issues such as higher wages, shorter hours, and better working conditions.*

4. **THE GREAT RAILROAD STRIKE, 1877**

   ▸ *Provoked by the Baltimore & Ohio Railroad's decision to cut wages for the second time in a year*

   ▸ *Remembered as the first general strike in American history*

   ▸ *Paralyzed the nation's commerce for 45 days*

   ▸ *Forced governors in ten states to mobilize 60,000 militia to reopen rail traffic*

5. **SHERMAN ANTITRUST ACT, 1890**

   ▸ *The act forbade only unreasonable combinations or contracts in restraint of trade.*

   ▸ *It had little immediate impact on the regulation of large corporations.*

   ▸ *During the last decade of the nineteenth century, the primary use of the act was to curb labor unions.*

   ▸ *The act declared illegal "every contract, combination in the form of trust, or otherwise, or conspiracy in restraint of trade among the several states."*

6. **HOMESTEAD STRIKE, 1892**

   ▸ *The strike began as a dispute between the Amalgamated Association of Iron and Steel Workers (the AA) and the Carnegie Steel Company.*

   ▸ *The AA refused to accept pay cuts and went on strike in Homestead, Pennsylvania.*

   ▸ *The strike ultimately culminated in a battle between strikers and private security guards hired by the company.*

7. THE PULLMAN STRIKE, 1894

▸ *During the late nineteenth century, the American labor movement experienced a number of violent strikes. The two best-known strikes were the Homestead Strike (1892) and the Pullman Strike (1894).*

▸ *When the national economy fell into a depression, the Pullman Palace Car Company cut wages while maintaining rents and prices in a company town where 12,000 workers lived. This action precipitated the Pullman Strike.*

▸ *The Pullman Strike halted a substantial portion of American railroad commerce.*

▸ *The strike ended when President Grover Cleveland ordered federal troops to Chicago, ostensibly to protect rail-carried mail but, in reality, to crush the strike.*

8. THE ANTHRACITE COAL STRIKE OF 1902

▸ *This was a strike by the United Mine Workers of America in the anthracite coal fields of eastern Pennsylvania.*

▸ *It was arbitrated with the active involvement of President Theodore Roosevelt; this marked the first time the federal government intervened in a labor dispute as a neutral arbitrator.*

9. THE WAGNER ACT OF 1935

▸ *The act is also known as the National Labor Relations Act.*

▸ *It is often called the Magna Carta of labor because it ensured workers' right to organize and bargain collectively.*

▸ *Passage of the act led to a dramatic increase in labor union membership.*

10. THE CONGRESS OF INDUSTRIAL WORKERS (CIO)

▸ *The CIO was led by John L. Lewis.*

▸ *The CIO organized unskilled and semiskilled factory workers in basic manufacturing industries such as steel and automobiles.*

▸ *Here is how John L. Lewis explained the goals and strategy of the CIO: "The productive methods and facilities of modern industry have been completely transformed. . . . Skilled artisans make up only a small proportion of the workers. Obviously the bargaining strength of employees under these conditions no longer rests in organizations of skilled craftsmen. It is dependent upon a national union representing all employees—whether skilled or unskilled, or whether working by brain or brawn—in each basic industry."*

11. **THE SPLIT BETWEEN THE AFL AND THE CIO**
  ▸ *The American Federation of Labor (AFL) split apart at its national convention in 1935.*
  ▸ *A majority of AFL leaders refused to grant charters to new unions organized on an industry-wide basis.*
  ▸ *The AFL favored the organization of workers according to their skills and trades.*
  ▸ *The CIO favored the organization of all workers in a particular industry.*

12. **TAFT-HARTLEY ACT, 1947**
  ▸ *The primary purpose was to curb the power of labor unions.*
  ▸ *Supporters of the Taft-Hartley Act believed the following:*
    (a) *Unions were abusing their power.*
    (b) *Widespread strikes would endanger the nation's vital defense industries.*
    (c) *Some labor unions had been infiltrated by Communists.*
    (d) *Employers were being coerced into hiring union workers.*
  ▸ *Organized labor opposed the Taft-Hartley Act.*

> *APUSH test writers frequently ask questions about the Wagner Act and the Taft-Hartley Act. The former helped organized labor by guaranteeing labor the right to organize and form unions. The latter was intended to curb the power of labor unions.*

13. **UNITED FARM WORKERS**
  ▸ *The workers were organized and led by César Chávez, Dolores Huerta, Philip Vera Cruz, and Larry Itliong.*
  ▸ *This was a union of farm workers.*
  ▸ *César Chávez is recognized as a significant civil rights leader.*

KEY FACTS ABOUT TWENTY ACTS OF CONGRESS

1. NAVIGATION ACTS, 1651
    ▶ *The acts put mercantilism into practice. Colonial products that could be shipped only to England were listed.*
    ▶ *The acts were designed to subordinate the colonial economy to that of the mother country.*

Test Tip

Don't overlook the Navigation Acts and mercantilism. They have appeared on almost every APUSH exam.

2. SUGAR ACT, 1764
    ▶ *The Sugar Act was the first law passed by Parliament to raise revenue for the British Crown.*
    ▶ *The Sugar Act was designed to tighten enforcement of English customs laws in America.*
    ▶ *Following bitter protests from the colonists, British officials lowered the duties.*

3. STAMP ACT, 1765
    ▶ *The primary purpose was to raise revenue to support British troops stationed in America.*
    ▶ *Issue raised: Does Parliament have the right to tax the colonies without their consent?*
    ▶ *The act was repealed because colonial boycotts of English goods were hurting British merchants.*
    ▶ *The act was important for the following reasons:*
        (a) *It revealed that many colonists believed they were entitled to all the rights and privileges of British subjects.*

(b) The colonists demonstrated their willingness to use violence rather than legal means to frustrate British policy.

(c) The British maintained that the colonies had no right to independence from parliamentary authority.

(d) Patriot leaders claimed that the act denied them their British birthrights.

4. COERCIVE ACTS, 1774

▶ The acts were the British response to the Boston Tea Party.

▶ They were widely known in the colonies as the Intolerable Acts.

▶ Parliament closed the port of Boston and drastically reduced the power of self-government in the Massachusetts colony.

▶ The Coercive Acts also provided for the quartering of troops in the colonists' barns and empty houses.

5. KANSAS-NEBRASKA ACT, 1854

▶ The act repealed the Missouri Compromise of 1820, thus heightening the sectional crisis.

▶ It applied the principle of popular sovereignty to the territories.

▶ It permitted the expansion of slavery beyond the Southern states.

▶ It sparked the formation of the Republican Party.

Test Tip

The Kansas-Nebraska Act was one of the most important acts in American history. Be sure you know that it repealed the Missouri Compromise of 1820, applied the principle of popular sovereignty to the territories, and galvanized the formation of the Republican Party.

6. HOMESTEAD ACT, 1862

▶ The act permitted any citizen or prospective citizen to claim 160 acres of public land and to purchase it for a small fee after living on it for five years.

▶ The Homestead Act played a role in encouraging the settlement of the Western frontier.

7. CHINESE EXCLUSION ACT OF 1882

▶ This was the first law to exclude a group from America because of ethnic background.

▶ It prohibited the immigration of Chinese to America.

▶ It was strongly supported by working-class Americans.

▶ It reflected anti-immigration sentiment in California.

8. DAWES ACT, 1887
    ▸ *The act divided Native American tribal lands into individual holdings.*
    ▸ *The purpose was to assimilate American Indians into the mainstream of American culture.*
    ▸ *Reflecting the forced-civilization views of the reformers, the act dissolved many tribes as legal entities, wiped out tribal ownership of land, and set up individual Indian family heads with 160 acres.*

9. SHERMAN ANTITRUST ACT, 1890
    ▸ *The act forbade unreasonable combinations or contracts in restraint of trade.*
    ▸ *It had little immediate impact on the regulation of large corporations.*
    ▸ *During the last decade of the nineteenth century, the primary use of the act was to curb labor unions.*

10. THE PURE FOOD AND DRUG ACT, 1906
    ▸ *The act was an example of Progressive Era legislation.*
    ▸ *It was prompted by the public outrage unleashed by the publication of Upton Sinclair's novel* The Jungle.

11. FEDERAL RESERVE ACT OF 1913
    ▸ *The act created a central Federal Reserve Board appointed by the President.*
    ▸ *It established a national system of 12 district banks, coordinated by a central board.*
    ▸ *The Federal Reserve System made currency and credit more elastic.*

Test Tip

Actions of the Federal Reserve Board spark headlines and heated debate. Although APUSH questions about the Federal Reserve Board do not spark debate, they do challenge unprepared students. Be certain you can identify the Federal Reserve Board.

12. NATIONAL ORIGINS ACT, 1924
    ▸ *The primary purpose was to restrict the flow of newcomers from Southern and Eastern Europe.*
    ▸ *It established immigrant quotas that discriminated against Southern and Eastern Europeans.*
    ▸ *This was the primary reason for the decrease in the numbers of Europeans immigrating to the United States in the 1920s.*

13. **NATIONAL INDUSTRIAL RECOVERY ACT, 1933**
    ▸ *The National Industrial Recovery Act (NRA) sought to combat the Great Depression by fostering government-business cooperation.*
    ▸ *The act allowed businesses to regulate themselves through codes of fair competition.*
    ▸ *The NRA did not succeed. In contrast, Social Security proved to be much more enduring.*

14. **NEUTRALITY ACTS, 1930s**
    ▸ *The acts were expressions of a commitment to isolationism.*
    ▸ *During the 1930s, isolationists drew support for their position from Washington's Farewell Address.*

15. **SOCIAL SECURITY ACT, 1935**
    ▸ *The Social Security Act was part of the New Deal program of reforms.*
    ▸ *The Social Security Act created a federal pension system funded by taxes on a worker's wages and by an equivalent contribution by employers.*
    ▸ *The aging of America since the 1970s is widely seen as threatening the long-term solvency of the Social Security system.*

16. **WAGNER ACT, 1935**
    ▸ *The act is also known as the National Labor Relations Act of 1935.*
    ▸ *It is also known as the Magna Carta of Labor because it ensured workers the right to organize and bargain collectively.*
    ▸ *It led to a rapid rise in labor union membership.*

17. **LEND-LEASE ACT, 1941**
    ▸ *The purpose of the Lend-Lease Act was to provide military supplies to the Allies.*
    ▸ *The Lend-Lease program was used primarily to help Great Britain and the Soviet Union resist Nazi Germany.*

18. **TAFT-HARTLEY ACT, 1947**
    ▸ *The primary purpose was to curb the power of labor unions.*
    ▸ *Supporters of the Taft-Hartley Act believed that unions were abusing their powers and that widespread strikes would endanger national defense industries.*
    ▸ *Organized labor opposed the Taft-Hartley Act.*

19. FEDERAL HIGHWAY ACT OF 1956
   ▸ *The act created the Interstate Highway System.*
   ▸ *It played a key role in promoting suburban growth.*

20. UNITED STATES IMMIGRATION AND NATIONALITY ACT OF 1965
   ▸ *The National Origins Acts of the 1920s severely restricted immigration into the United States.*
   ▸ *The United States Immigration and Nationality Act of 1965 abolished the national-origins quota system.*

PEOPLE in MOTION: IMMIGRATION and MIGRATION

 I. THE COLONIAL PERIOD

A. THE PURITANS

1. The Puritans immigrated to New England in the 1630s for the following reasons:
   - ▶ *A desire to escape political repression*
   - ▶ *A desire to find new economic opportunities and avoid an economic recession in England*
   - ▶ *A desire to escape restrictions on their religious practices*

2. The Puritans who immigrated to New England were part of what is known as the Great English Migration that numbered some 70,000 people. It is interesting to note that over twice as many Puritans immigrated to the West Indies as to New England.

B. MIGRATION TO APPALACHIA

1. The Proclamation of 1763 set a boundary along the crest of the Appalachians beyond which the colonists could not cross. The ban was an ill-considered attempt to prevent costly conflicts with trans-Appalachian Indians.

2. As American Indians were defeated, Scotch-Irish, German, and English immigrants moved into Appalachia.

3. British colonists were principally motivated to settle west of the Appalachians by the low price and easy availability of land.

American settlers ignored the Proclamation of 1763, and so do many APUSH students. APUSH test writers, however, have not ignored the Proclamation of 1763. They have written a surprising number of questions to see if APUSH students remember the purpose of this often forgotten boundary.

II. THE EARLY NINETEENTH CENTURY: 1800–1850

A. THE IRISH

1. Ireland supplied the largest number of immigrants to the United States during the first half of the nineteenth century.
2. The Irish fled the devastating effects of the potato famine.
3. Most Irish immigrants settled in urban cities along the Eastern Seaboard.
4. Many Irish immigrants worked on canal and railroad construction projects.

B. THE GERMANS

1. Germany supplied the second-largest number of immigrants to the United States during the first half of the nineteenth century.
2. Many Germans were fleeing political turmoil in their homeland.

C. THE KNOW-NOTHING PARTY

1. The Know-Nothings were America's first nativist political party.
2. The Know-Nothings directed their hostility against Catholic immigrants from Ireland and Germany.

III. THE LATE NINETEENTH AND EARLY TWENTIETH CENTURY: 1880–1924

A. EXODUSTERS

1. Exodusters were African Americans who fled the violence of the Reconstruction South in 1879 and 1880.
2. Most Exodusters migrated to Kansas.

B. THE NEW IMMIGRANTS

1. Prior to 1880, most immigrants to the United States came from the British Isles and Western Europe.

2. Beginning in the 1880s, a new wave of immigrants left Europe for America. The so-called New Immigrants came from small towns and villages in Southern and Eastern Europe. The majority immigrated from Italy, Russia, Poland, and Austria-Hungary.

3. The New Immigrants primarily settled in large cities in the Northeast and Midwest.

4. Very few New Immigrants settled in the South.

C. THE CHINESE EXCLUSION ACT of 1882

1. This was the first law in American history to exclude a group because of ethnic background.

2. The act prohibited the immigration of Chinese to America.

3. It was strongly supported by working-class Americans.

4. It reflected anti-immigration sentiment in California.

D. NATIVIST OPPOSITION TO THE NEW IMMIGRANTS

1. Nativists opposed the New Immigrants of the late nineteenth and early twentieth centuries for the following reasons:
   - *The New Immigrants practiced different religions.*
   - *The New Immigrants had different languages and cultures.*
   - *The New Immigrants were willing to work for lower wages than native-born workers.*
   - *The New Immigrants were not familiar with the American political system.*

E. THE NATIONAL ORIGINS ACT

1. The primary purpose of the National Origins Act was to use quotas to restrict the flow of newcomers from Southern and Eastern Europe.

2. The quotas favored immigration from Northern and Western Europe.

KEY THEMES AND FACTS

3. The quotas established by the National Origins Act discriminated against immigrants from Southern and Eastern Europe. These quotas were the primary reason for the decrease in the numbers of Europeans immigrating to the United States in the 1920s.
4. The number of Mexicans and Puerto Ricans immigrating to the United States increased because neither group was affected by the restrictive immigration acts of 1921 and 1924.

IV. THE BLACK MIGRATION

A. CAUSES

1. Jim Crow laws denied African Americans their rights as citizens and forced them to endure poverty and systematic discrimination.
2. Beginning with World War I, the wartime demand for labor attracted African Americans to cities in the North and West.
3. The Black migration to the cities of the North and West continued during World War II.

B. LEAVING THE RURAL SOUTH

1. In 1915, the overwhelming majority of African Americans lived in the rural South.
2. Attracted by the wartime demand for labor, African Americans migrated to urban centers in the North and West.

V. IMMIGRATION FROM MEXICO

A. THE DEPRESSION

1. During the Great Depression, many Mexicans returned to their homeland.

B. SURGE IN MEXICAN IMMIGRATION

1. The following factors played an important role in Mexican immigration to the United States during the twentieth century:

▸ The relaxation of immigration quotas during the 1960s
▸ The desire to escape a crowded homeland with few economic opportunities
▸ The desire to take advantage of better job opportunities in the United States
▸ The desire to reunite with family members who had previously immigrated to the United States

VI. POPULATION SHIFTS AFTER WORLD WAR II

A. FROM CITIES TO SUBURBS

1. The 1950s witnessed the beginning of a mass migration of middle-income Americans from cities to their surrounding suburbs.

2. The movement to the suburbs was facilitated by the construction of the interstate highway system.

B. FROM THE FROSTBELT TO THE SUNBELT

1. Beginning in the 1970s, the largest growth in population occurred in states below the 37th parallel, from Virginia to California.

2. The 1970s witnessed a significant migration of Americans from the Frostbelt to the Sunbelt. This migration has continued to the present.

3. The South and West have experienced the greatest population gains since 1970.

C. FROM LATIN AMERICA AND ASIA TO AMERICA

1. The last 25 years have witnessed a significant increase in immigration from Latin America and Asia.

2. Latinos now make up nearly 33 percent of the population in Texas, Arizona, and California; they make up 40 percent in New Mexico.

Test Tip

Most APUSH exams have very few questions on the period since 1980. When APUSH test writers do cover the last three decades, they often ask questions about the population shifts and demographic trends discussed in this section.

KEY THEMES AND FACTS

MILESTONES in U.S. FOREIGN POLICY: LATIN AMERICA

 I. THE MONROE DOCTRINE

A. REASONS THE MONROE DOCTRINE WAS ISSUED

1. The Monroe Doctrine was intended to do the following:
   - ▶ *Warn France, Russia, and Spain against further colonization or intervention in the New World*
   - ▶ *Express opposition to further European colonization in the New World*
   - ▶ *Protect republican institutions of government in the New World*
   - ▶ *Express America's intent to refrain from involvement in European rivalries*
   - ▶ *Assert American independence in foreign policy*

B. PRINCIPLES OF THE MONROE DOCTRINE

1. The Monroe Doctrine was a unilateral declaration of the following principles:
   - ▶ *Europe and the Western Hemisphere have essentially different political systems.*
   - ▶ *The American continents are no longer open to European colonization.*
   - ▶ *The United States will regard European interference in the political affairs of the Western Hemisphere as hostile behavior.*
   - ▶ *The United States will protect republican institutions of government in the Western Hemisphere.*
   - ▶ *The United States will not interfere in the internal affairs of European nations.*

C. ROLE OF THE BRITISH NAVY

1. The United States lacked the military power to enforce the Monroe Doctrine.
2. However, the principles expressed in the Monroe Doctrine were consistent with British foreign policy goals.
3. Although the British did not formally endorse the Monroe Doctrine, their navy was a de facto enforcer of its principles.

II. THE SPANISH-AMERICAN WAR

A. CAUSES OF THE WAR

1. The battleship USS *Maine* was sunk mysteriously in Havana harbor.
2. There was a circulation battle between the "yellow journalism" newspapers of Joseph Pulitzer and William Randolph Hearst. The sensational stories in both newspapers played a significant role in arousing public support for a war to liberate Cuba and avenge the sinking of the *Maine*.

B. TERRITORIAL ACQUISITIONS

1. As a result of the Spanish-American War, Spain relinquished to the United States control of the following:
   - *Guam*
   - *Puerto Rico*
   - *Cuba*
   - *The Philippines*
2. When the United States established a protectorate over Cuba, it practiced imperialism.

C. THE DEBATE OVER ANNEXING THE PHILIPPINES

1. The Anti-Imperialism League opposed annexation, arguing that it violated America's long-established commitment to the principles of self-determination and anticolonialism.
2. Supporters of annexation argued that America had a moral responsibility to "civilize" the islands. They also pointed out that the Philippines could become a valuable trading partner.

III. THE ROOSEVELT COROLLARY TO THE MONROE DOCTRINE

A. REASONS THE ROOSEVELT COROLLARY WAS ISSUED

1. President Theodore Roosevelt worried that the Dominican Republic and other Latin American nations would default on debts owed to European banks. These defaults could then provoke European military intervention.

2. Roosevelt issued the Roosevelt Corollary to the Monroe Doctrine to forestall European intervention.

B. PRINCIPLES AND CONSEQUENCES OF THE COROLLARY

1. The Roosevelt Corollary asserted America's right to intervene in the affairs of Central America and the Caribbean.

2. It expanded America's role in Central America and the Caribbean.

3. It claimed America's right to act as an international police power in Central and South America. Presidents Roosevelt, Taft, and Wilson enforced the Roosevelt Corollary by sending American troops to Cuba, Panama, Nicaragua, the Dominican Republic, Mexico, and Haiti.

4. Here is how Theodore Roosevelt explained and justified the Roosevelt Corollary:

   "Chronic wrongdoing, or an impotence which results in a general loosening of the ties of civilized society, may in America, as elsewhere, ultimately require intervention by some civilized nation, and in the Western Hemisphere the adherence of the United States to the Monroe Doctrine may force the United States . . . to the exercise of an international police power."

The Monroe Doctrine and the Roosevelt Corollary are two of the most frequently tested topics on the APUSH exam. Make sure that you carefully study this list of key points for both of these foreign policies.

IV. DOLLAR DIPLOMACY

A. REASONS FOR DOLLAR DIPLOMACY

1. During the presidency of William Howard Taft, U.S. policy in Latin America was primarily driven by concerns for U.S. economic and strategic interests in the region.

B. AN EXAMPLE OF DOLLAR DIPLOMACY

1. William Howard Taft's use of American bankers to refinance the foreign debt of Nicaragua exemplifies Dollar Diplomacy.

V. THE GOOD NEIGHBOR POLICY

A. REASONS FOR THE GOOD NEIGHBOR POLICY

1. The United States sought greater cooperation with the nations of Latin America, primarily to develop a hemispheric common front against Fascism.

B. PRINCIPLES OF THE GOOD NEIGHBOR POLICY

1. The Roosevelt administration formally renounced U.S. armed intervention in the affairs of Latin America.
2. As part of its Good Neighbor policy, the United States participated in reciprocal trade agreements with nations in Latin America.

VI. THE ALLIANCE FOR PROGRESS

A. REASONS FOR THE ALLIANCE FOR PROGRESS

1. The Alliance for Progress was initiated by President John F. Kennedy in 1961. It aimed to establish economic cooperation between North America and South America.
2. The Alliance for Progress was intended to counter the emerging Communist threat from Cuba.

B. RESULTS OF THE ALLIANCE

1. The Alliance for Progress was a brief public relations success.
2. Although there were some limited economic gains, the Alliance for Progress was widely viewed as a failure.
3. The Organization of American States disbanded the Alliance for Progress in 1973.

Although most students are keenly aware of the Monroe Doctrine and the Roosevelt Corollary, few can identify FDR's Good Neighbor Policy and JFK's Alliance for Progress. Both initiatives were short-lived and had few lasting consequences. Don't fall into the trap of neglecting these topics, however. APUSH test writers have an uncanny knack for remembering topics that students often forget.

VII. KENNEDY AND CUBA

A. THE BAY OF PIGS

1. President Kennedy inherited from the Eisenhower administration a CIA-backed scheme to topple Fidel Castro from power by invading Cuba with anti-Communist exiles.
2. When the invasion failed, Kennedy refused to rescue the insurgents, forcing them to surrender.
3. Widely denounced as a fiasco, the Bay of Pigs defeat damaged U.S. credibility.
4. The Bay of Pigs failure, along with continuing American covert efforts to assassinate Castro, pushed the Cuban dictator into an even closer alliance with the Soviet Union.
5. Soviet Premier Khrushchev responded by secretly sending nuclear missiles to Cuba.

B. THE CUBAN MISSILE CRISIS

1. The Cuban Missile Crisis was precipitated by the discovery of Soviet missile sites in Cuba.
2. As part of the negotiations to end the Cuban Missile Crisis, President Kennedy promised to refrain from a military invasion of Cuba.

MILESTONES IN U.S. FOREIGN POLICY: THE VIETNAM WAR

I. THE ROAD TO VIETNAM

A. POLICY OF CONTAINMENT

1. Following World War II, the United States adopted the policy of containment to halt the expansion of Communist influence.

2. American involvement in Vietnam grew out of the policy commitments and assumptions of containment.

B. THE FRENCH WITHDRAWAL

1. Following World War II, the French continued to exercise influence and control over Indochina.

2. The Viet Minh defeated the French at the pivotal Battle of Dienbienphu in 1954. Following their defeat, the French withdrew from Vietnam.

3. The United States refused to sign the Geneva Accords and soon replaced the French as the dominant Western power in Indochina.

C. THE DOMINO EFFECT

1. The United States believed that if one nation fell under Communist control, nearby nations would inevitably also fall under Communist influence.

2. Here is how Secretary of State Dean Rusk explained the domino effect:

"If Indo-China were to fall and if its fall led to the loss of all of Southeast Asia, then the United States might eventually be forced back to Hawaii, as it was before the Second World War."

II. THE TONKIN GULF RESOLUTION, 1964

A. AN INCIDENT IN THE GULF OF TONKIN

1. The United States alleged that North Vietnamese torpedo boats launched an unprovoked attack against American destroyers in the Gulf of Tonkin.
2. The facts of what actually happened have never been fully explained.

B. THE RESOLUTION

1. Congress responded to the unsubstantiated report of North Vietnamese aggression by overwhelmingly passing the Tonkin Gulf Resolution.
2. The resolution authorized President Lyndon Johnson to "take all necessary measures to repel any armed attack against the forces of the United States and to prevent further aggression."
3. The Tonkin Gulf Resolution gave President Johnson a blank check to escalate the war in Vietnam.
4. Within a short time, President Johnson began to dramatically escalate the number of U.S. troops in Vietnam.

> *The Vietnam War was both long and complex. Despite the war's complexity, APUSH test writers only focus on a few key points. The Tonkin Gulf Resolution is a pivotal turning point that you absolutely, positively have to know. In essence, the resolution gave President Johnson a blank check to escalate the war.*

III. THE TET OFFENSIVE, 1968

A. WHAT HAPPENED?

1. In late January 1968, the Viet Cong suddenly launched a series of attacks on 27 key South Vietnamese cities, including the capital, Saigon.
2. The Viet Cong were eventually forced to retreat after suffering heavy losses.

B. CONSEQUENCES

1. The Tet Offensive undermined President Johnson's credibility.
2. As a result of the Tet Offensive, public support for the war decreased and antiwar sentiment increased.

IV. HAWKS AND DOVES

A. HAWKS AND THE SILENT MAJORITY

1. Hawks supported the Vietnam War.
2. The Silent Majority was the name given by President Nixon to the moderate, mainstream Americans who quietly supported his Vietnam War policies. Members of the Silent Majority believed that the United States was justified in supporting South Vietnam.

B. DOVES

1. Doves opposed the Vietnam War.
2. Senator William Fulbright was a leading Dove. He wrote a critique of the war entitled *The Arrogance of Power*.

V. THE INVASION OF CAMBODIA AND KENT STATE, 1970

A. VIETNAMIZATION

1. Supported by the Silent Majority, Nixon began to slowly withdraw American troops from Vietnam and replace them with newly trained South Vietnamese troops.
2. Known as Vietnamization, the policy promised to preserve U.S. goals and bring "peace with honor."

B. THE INVASION OF CAMBODIA

1. On April 29, 1970, President Nixon suddenly and without consulting Congress ordered American forces to join with the South Vietnamese army in cleaning out the Viet Cong sanctuaries in officially neutral Cambodia.

2. Nixon defended the action, saying that it was necessary to protect American forces and support Vietnamization.

C. KENT STATE

1. Angry students responded to the Cambodian invasion with demonstrations at campuses across the United States.

2. At Kent State University in Ohio, nervous members of the National Guard fired into a noisy crowd, killing four students and wounding many more.

Test Tip

Recent APUSH exams have included questions about the invasion of Cambodia and the shootings at Kent State. Remember, the invasion of Cambodia was motivated by a desire to destroy Viet Cong sanctuaries in neutral Cambodia, thus protecting Nixon's policy of Vietnamization. The shootings at Kent State were an unexpected consequence of the Cambodian invasion.

VI. CONSEQUENCES OF THE VIETNAM WAR

A. THE WAR AND THE ECONOMY

1. The United States could not afford both President Johnson's Great Society programs and the Vietnam War.

2. The combination of spending on the war and social programs produced the high inflation rates of the late 1960s and early 1970s.

B. THE WAR AND INTERNATIONAL INVOLVEMENT

1. The Vietnam War increased public skepticism toward international involvement.

2. In 1973, Congress passed the War Powers Act, placing restrictions on a president's ability to wage wars.

PART IV:

TEST-TAKING STRATEGIES

STRATEGIES FOR THE MULTIPLE-CHOICE QUESTIONS

Your APUSH exam will begin with a 55-minute section containing 80 multiple-choice questions. These questions typically begin with the founding of Jamestown in 1607 and end with Reaganomics in the early 1980s. There may be a general question or two about major demographic trends since the 1980s.

Each multiple-choice question is worth 1.125 points. The 80 multiple-choice questions are thus worth a total of 90 points or half of the 180 points that are on the APUSH exam. Beginning with the May 2011 administration of the APUSH exam, the College Board has changed the scoring of the multiple-choice section. The score achieved on the multiple-choice section of the exam will be based on the number of questions answered correctly. Points will no longer be deducted for incorrect answers or unanswered questions.

With this change, the "guessing penalty" is eliminated, but don't waste precious time. If you do not have any idea how to answer a question, skip it and move on. If you can eliminate two or more answers, you should use the process of elimination to take an educated guess.

A GRAND STRATEGY

The multiple-choice questions are vital to achieving a high score. Although they account for just under one-third of the APUSH exam's total time, they are worth 50 percent of the exam's total points. Never forget that on the 2006 exam you only needed 111 points to score a 5 and 91 points to score a 4.

The multiple-choice questions cover very predictable topics. At least one-fourth of the questions will be devoted to African American and women's history. Another ten questions will cover key terms and key

Supreme Court cases and trials. In addition, most exams devote four to six questions to charts, political cartoons, pictures, and maps. These graphic questions are particularly straightforward, since all of the information you need is provided in the chart, cartoon, picture, or map.

Chapters 2–32 in this book contain all of the information you will need to ace the multiple-choice questions. If you carefully review these chapters, you should be able to correctly answer at least 60 of the 80 multiple-choice questions. If you miss 12 questions and leave 8 blank, this will give you a raw score of 67.50 points. You will then only need another 43.50 points to score a 5 and just 23.50 points to score a 4!

TWO CHALLENGING FORMATS

Most APUSH multiple-choice questions are straightforward. However, test writers do use two formats that require closer examination:

"EXCEPT" QUESTIONS

Between six and eight questions on each exam will provide you with four answers that are correct and one answer that is incorrect. Known as EXCEPT questions, these problems ask you to find the answer that does not fit or is incorrect. The best strategy is to treat these questions as if they were five-part true-false questions. Simply go through the question and label each answer choice "true" or "false." The correct answer is the one that is false. Here are three examples:

1. **Booker T. Washington stressed the importance of all of the following EXCEPT**

    (A) *pursuing vocational education*

    (B) *developing racial solidarity*

    (C) *avoiding public protests*

    (D) *integrating restaurants and schools*

    (E) *gaining Black political power*

    Answer choices A, B, C, and D are all true. Since only E is false, it is the correct answer. Booker T. Washington advocated a policy of racial accommodation and economic self-help.

He stressed the importance of avoiding a struggle for political power.

2. **All of the following reformers are correctly paired with the reform issue with which they were most involved EXCEPT**

    (A) *Ida B. Wells . . . lynching in the South*

    (B) *Betty Friedan . . . gender roles*

    (C) *Dorothea Dix . . . women's suffrage*

    (D) *Margaret Sanger . . . birth control*

    (E) *Rachel Carson . . . overuse of chemical insecticides*

Answer choices A, B, D, and E are all true. Since only C is false, it is the correct answer. Dorothea Dix focused her attention on reforming the condition and treatment of the mentally ill. She was not actively involved in the fight for women's rights.

3. **All of the following were accomplishments of the New Deal EXCEPT**

    (A) *desegregating the armed forces*

    (B) *granting labor the right to organize and bargain collectively*

    (C) *establishing short-term programs to reduce unemployment*

    (D) *reforming aspects of the nation's banking system and stock market*

    (E) *creating a Social Security system financed by a payroll tax on both employees and employers*

Answer choices B, C, D, and E are all true. Since only A is false, it is the correct answer. President Truman desegregated the armed forces in 1948.

QUOTE QUESTIONS

Between three to four questions on each exam will provide you with a quote and ask you to link the quote to a key person, term, or document. Many of the quotes are well known, while others are not. Regardless of whether the quote is famous or obscure, it will have a key word, phrase, or definition that will clearly establish its purpose. Your job is to find the key parts of the quote and connect them to the answer. Here are three examples:

1. **"The very basis of our individual rights and freedoms rests upon the certainty that the President and the Executive Branch of government will support and insure the carrying out of the decisions of the federal courts, even, when necessary, with all the means at the President's command."**

    This statement was most likely made by which of the following Presidents and under what circumstances?

    (A) *Andrew Jackson, as he sent troops to enforce the Supreme Court's decision in* Worcester v. Georgia

    (B) *Theodore Roosevelt, as he sent troops to end the Anthracite Coal Strike*

    (C) *Franklin Roosevelt, as he sent troops to evict the Bonus Expeditionary Force*

    (D) *Dwight Eisenhower, as he sent troops to Little Rock to enforce desegregation orders*

    (E) *John F. Kennedy, as he sent troops to assist Governor Wallace's promise to block the admission of Black students to the University of Alabama*

    The key phrase in this quote states that the President "will support and insure the carrying out of the decisions of the federal courts." You therefore should look for an answer in which a president used troops to carry out a court order. Choice A can be eliminated since Andrew Jackson refused to carry out the Supreme Court's decision in *Worcester v. Georgia*. Choice B can be eliminated since Theodore Roosevelt used arbitration to settle the Anthracite Coal Strike. Choice C can be eliminated since Herbert Hoover, not Franklin Roosevelt, used force to evict the Bonus Marchers. And finally, choice E can be eliminated since John F. Kennedy did not send troops to support Governor Wallace. President Kennedy did send troops to Oxford, Mississippi. Only choice D is correct.

2. **"When the people elected Tammany, they knew just what they were doin'. We didn't put up any false pretenses. We didn't go in for humbug civil service and all that rot. We stood as we have always stood, for rewardin' the men that won the victory. . . . When we go in, we fire every anti-Tammany man from office that can be fired under the law."**

   In the statement above, a New York City politician defends

   (A) *the Electoral College*

   (B) *the system of checks and balances*

   (C) *Civil Service reform*

   (D) *initiative, recall, and referendum*

   (E) *the spoils system*

   The key phrase in this quote states, "We stood as we have always stood, for rewardin' the men that won the victory." Rewarding the victors would clearly indicate that the New York City politician is defending the spoils system. Choice E is the answer.

3. **"Our policy is directed not against any country or doctrine, but against hunger, poverty, desperation, and chaos. Its purpose should be the revival of a working economy in the world so as to permit the emergence of political and social conditions in which free institutions can exist. . . . Any government that is willing to assist in the task of recovery will find full cooperation, I am sure, on the part of the United States government."**

The passage expresses the rationale for

    (A) *the Monroe Doctrine*

    (B) *the Open Door Policy*

    (C) *Dollar Diplomacy*

    (D) *the Marshall Plan*

    (E) *the Camp David Accords*

The key phrase in this quote states that "Its purpose should be the revival of a working economy in the world so as to permit the emergence of political and social conditions in which free institutions can exist." The goal of reviving the global economy in the name of promoting free institutions clearly indicates that the passage is taken from the Marshall Plan. Choice D is the correct answer.

STRATEGIES FOR THE DOCUMENT-BASED ESSAY QUESTION

After completing the multiple-choice section, you will have a well-deserved ten-minute break. When you return to your desks, your exam will resume with the DBQ essay. (*DBQ* stands for document-based essay question.) The DBQ is an essay question that requires you to interpret and analyze nine or ten brief primary-source documents. The documents typically include a graph, map, or political cartoon, as well as excerpts from diaries, speeches, and legislative acts.

The DBQ begins with a mandatory 15-minute reading period. You should use this time to read the documents, organize your thoughts, determine a thesis, and prepare an outline for your essay. You will then have 45 minutes to write your essay.

Your DBQ essay will be scored on a 1-to-9 scale. Here are the scoring guidelines used by College Board readers:

8–9: Essay contains a well-developed thesis supported by a number of documents and substantial and relevant outside information.

5–7: Essay contains a consistent thesis supported by some documents and some relevant outside information.

2–4: Essay contains a partially developed thesis supported by brief references to the documents and little or no outside information.

0–1: Essay contains a confused thesis that shows inadequate or incorrect understanding of the questions and documents. The essay contains no outside information and may include substantial factual errors.

Each point on the 1-to-9 scale is worth 4.5 points. So a perfect score of 9 is worth 40.5 points, a 6 is worth 27 points, and a 4 is worth 18 points. It is very important to note the significance of outside information. Essays that lack outside information will not receive a score above 4.

The DBQ causes many students a great deal of anxiety. The question is impossible to predict, and the documents are often taken from unfamiliar sources. Although this is true, it is important to remember that the questions always cover subjects taken from the topical outline. The documents are brief and almost always easy to understand.

PRACTICE MATERIALS

Practice is key to performing well on the DBQ. Although practice will not necessarily lead to a perfect score, it will help you earn a high score. College Board materials are the best source of practice DBQs. The *2006 AP United States History Released Exam* and the *2001 AP United States History Released Exam* both include actual DBQs and scored sample essays. The College Board book *Doing the DBQ* includes 22 DBQs. All three of these booklets can be purchased from the College Board's online store. In addition, you should go to the AP United States History Course Homepage at AP Central. You'll find DBQs and sample essays from 1999 to the present.

STRATEGIES FOR SUCCESS

Using authentic practice materials is important. Following good strategies is essential. This section will use the DBQ from the 2008 APUSH exam to provide you with a guided set of strategies that can be used for any DBQ.

1. **Carefully analyze the assignment.**

   Begin your 15-minute mandatory reading period by carefully examining the assignment. The 2008 DBQ asked students to "Analyze the ways in which the Vietnam War heightened social, political, and economic tensions in the United States between 1964 and 1975." The assignment is asking you to analyze the cause-and-effect relationship between the Vietnam War and three specific types of heightened tensions— social, political, and economic.

2. **Carefully examine each document and create an organizational chart.**

   Your next step is to read, analyze, and organize the documents. The 2008 DBQ included the following nine documents:

   A. *An excerpt from the Tonkin Gulf Resolution, 1964*

   B. *Lyrics from the song "I-Feel-Like-I'm-Fixin'-To-Die," 1965*

   C. *An excerpt from a speech by Martin Luther King Jr. criticizing the Vietnam War, 1967*

   D. *A political cartoon showing that President Johnson's foreign policy was taking funds from his Great Society domestic programs, 1967*

   E. *An excerpt from a speech by Senator Robert F. Kennedy criticizing the Vietnam War, 1968*

   F. *An excerpt by a student describing how college students evaded the draft while working-class young men were drafted, 1969*

   G. *An excerpt from President Nixon's "Silent Majority" speech, 1969*

   H. *An excerpt from Senator McGovern criticizing the Vietnam War and defense strategy, 1972*

   I. *An excerpt from the War Powers Act, 1973*

   Many students find it very helpful to organize the documents by placing them into a chart. Since your assignment asks you to analyze social, political, and economic tensions, you should create a chart using these headings. Here is an example of what your chart could look like:

Document	Social	Political	Economic
A.		Yes	
B.	Yes		Yes
C.	Yes		Yes
D.			Yes
E.		Yes	
F.	Yes		Yes
G.		Yes	
H.		Yes	
I.		Yes	

The chart clearly identifies the political documents while also showing that there is a relationship between social and economic tensions.

3. Carefully write down outside information.

After reading the documents, pause and brain-storm potential outside information triggered by the documents. This is a crucial step. Remember, if you do not include outside information, your score will be no higher than 4. Given the importance of outside information, it is vital that you clearly and systematically organize your thoughts. Here is a revised chart with possible outside information listed in a separate column:

Document	Social	Political	Economic	Outside Information
A.		Yes		Containment, Escalation, Domino theory
B.	Yes		Yes	Counterculture, Generation Gap, Hippies
C.	Yes		Yes	War on Poverty, rise of Black militancy
D.			Yes	War on Poverty
E.		Yes		Tet Offensive, Credibility Gap, Election of 1968

F.	Yes		Yes	Hawks and Doves, Generation Gap
G.		Yes		Vietnamization, Polarized society, Hawks and Doves
H.		Yes		Inflation
I.		Yes		New Isolationism, End of imperial presidency

4. Carefully determine your thesis.

A thesis statement is your position on the assigned topic. Having a clearly defined and focused thesis is absolutely essential. If you have not fully formulated your thesis during the 15-minute mandatory thinking period, do not panic. There is no rule saying that you must begin writing after the 15 minutes are up. It is better to take a few extra minutes to mentally work on your thesis than to rush and end up with a weak thesis.

Here is a sample thesis statement for the 2008 DBQ:

In August 1964 Congress overwhelmingly approved the Tonkin Gulf Resolution (Document A), giving President Johnson a blank check to escalate the Vietnam War. At that time, there were only about 24,000 American advisors in South Vietnam. Americans enjoyed economic prosperity and shared a consensus on the wisdom of containment and the validity of the domino theory.

President Johnson enjoyed great popularity and prepared to launch his Great Society programs and ambitious War on Poverty. The dramatic escalation of the Vietnam War shattered America's political consensus, ended the dominance of the Democratic Party, and weakened the Imperial Presidency. At the same time, the war triggered an inflationary spiral while polarizing American society into an increasingly alienated counterculture and an increasingly angry "Silent Majority."

5. **Carefully write the rest of your essay.**

    Now that you have written a strong thesis, your final step is to finish your essay. As you write your essay, be sure to effectively analyze several documents while incorporating as much relevant outside information as you can. Your chart will be a handy reference that will keep you focused and prevent you from making unnecessary digressions.

STRATEGIES FOR THE FREE-RESPONSE ESSAYS

After completing your DBQ, you will yearn for a break to rest your tired writing hand. Unfortunately, there is no break. Instead, you must be resolute and focus on the next and final APUSH challenge—the free-response essays.

You will have 70 minutes to complete two free-response essays. The free-response essays are grouped into two sets. Part B of your exam contains two essay questions that cover pre-Civil War topics. Part C of your exam contains two essay questions that cover post-Civil War topics. The directions ask you to choose one question from Part B and one question from Part C.

Each free-response question will be scored on a 1-to-9 scale. Here are the scoring guidelines used by College Board readers:

8–9: Essay contains a clear, well-developed thesis supported with considerable relevant historical information.

5–7: Essay contains a partially developed thesis supported with some relevant historical information.

2–4: Essay contains a confused and unfocused thesis supported with few relevant facts.

0–1: Essay lacks a thesis and demonstrates little or no understanding of the question.

Each point on the 1-to-9 scale is worth 2.75 points. So a perfect score of 9 is worth 24.75 points, a 6 is worth 16.50 points, and a 4 is worth 11 points. The two free-response essays are worth a combined total of 49.50 points.

PRACTICE MATERIALS

Practice is key to performing well on the free-response essays. Although practice will not guarantee a perfect score, it will help you earn a high score. The *2006 AP United States History Released Exam* and the *2001 AP United States History Released Exam* both include actual free-response questions and scored sample essays. Both booklets can be purchased from the College Board's online store. In addition, you should visit the AP United States History Course Homepage at AP Central (*www.apcentral.collegeboard.com*). You will find a full set of free-response questions and sample essays from 1999 to the present.

STRATEGIES FOR SUCCESS

Using authentic practice materials is important. Following good strategies is essential. This section will discuss six strategies that will help you achieve high scores on your free-response essays:

1. **Make pragmatic choices.**

   Your first task is to select which of the two questions in Part B and Part C you want to write on. Above all, make a pragmatic or practical choice. Use the five-minute planning period before each part to carefully evaluate the two questions. Always choose the question that you know the most about.

2. **Anticipate questions *without* categories and questions with categories.**

   Your pragmatic choice may be influenced by the presence of two types of questions. One type is direct and lacks subcategories. For example, one recent question asked students to evaluate the groups of people who benefited from the opportunities in the Old West. The second question in the set asked students to discuss how two of the following three factors helped shape American culture in the 1920s: advertising, entertainment, and mass production. Which question would you choose to answer? If you have a weak understanding of the American West question but have a good knowledge of at least one of the three listed factors shaping American culture in the

1920s, you should choose the second question. Remember, when you are asked to choose from two of three categories, each one is worth 12.375 points. So don't despair if you can only write about one category. Do your best, pick up as many points as you can, and move on to the next set of questions. It is interesting to note that about 60 percent of all free-response questions have sub-categories.

3. **Make African American and women's history a priority.**

A comprehensive knowledge of African American and women's history is essential to achieving a high score on the APUSH exam. Chapter 33 stressed that at least one-fourth of the multiple-choice questions are devoted to these two topics. A similar pattern also appears on the free-response essays, in which two out of every five questions are devoted, in whole or in part, to African American and women's history. For a complete review of these topics, see Chapters 22–24.

4. **Study Native American history.**

A knowledge of Native American history is also very valuable on the free-response essays. About one of every eight free-response questions is, in whole or in part, devoted to this topic. Be sure to review Chapter 25, "Milestones in Native American History." There is a 50-50 chance your exam will have a free-response question that includes an aspect of Native American history.

5. **Write a clear, well-developed thesis.**

Remember, a thesis statement is your position on the question. Writing a clear, well-developed thesis statement is essential to earning a high score. Make sure that your thesis fully addresses the question. For example, the 2006 APUSH exam included a free-response question asking students to analyze the critiques of United States society in the 1950s by two of the following: youth, civil rights activists, and intellectuals. Here is a clear, fully developed thesis statement for this question:

Consensus and conformity dominated American society during the 1950s. Americans lived in mass-produced suburbs where women returned to traditional gender roles and children watched homogenized television shows in which everyone looked alike. But not everyone in America liked Ike or loved Lucy. Led by Rosa Parks, Martin Luther King Jr., and Thurgood Marshall, civil rights activists began to challenge Jim Crow segregation. At the same time, Beat writers such as Jack Kerouac questioned the value of middle-class conformity, and singers such as Little Richard and Elvis Presley pioneered a new and rebellious style of music called rock and roll.

6. **Carefully write the rest of your essay.**

Now that you have written a strong thesis, your final step is to finish your essay. As you write your essay, be sure to include as much relevant supporting historical evidence as you can.